REVIVING THE AMERICAN SPIRIT

REVIVING THE AMERICAN SPIRIT

KEITH BUTLER

FRONT LINE

A STRANG COMPANY

Most STRANG COMMUNICATIONS/CHARISMA HOUSE/SILOAM/
FRONTLINE products are available at special quantity discounts
for bulk purchase for sales promotions, premiums, fund-raising,
and educational needs. For details, write Strang Communications/
Charisma House/Siloam/FrontLine, 600 Rinehart Road, Lake Mary,
Florida 32746, or telephone (407) 333-0600.

REVIVING THE AMERICAN SPIRIT by Keith Butler
Published by FrontLine
A Strang Company
600 Rinehart Road
Lake Mary, Florida 32746
www.frontlineissues.com

Scripture quotations marked NRSV are from the New Revised
Standard Version of the Bible. Copyright © 1989 by the Division of
Christian Education of the National Council of Churches of Christ
in the USA. Used by permission.

Cover design by Judith McKittrick
Interior design by Terry Clifton

Library of Congress Cataloging-in-Publication Data:
An application to register this book for cataloginzg has been submitted to the Library of Congress.
International Standard Book Number: 1-59185-963-8 (hardback);
1-59185-964-6 (trade paper)

First Edition

06 07 08 09 10 — 987654321
Printed in the United States of America

CONTENTS

PREFACE: COMMON SENSE ix

1 BLACK AND REPUBLICAN 1

2 THE MORALITY CONNECTION 19

3 IN DEFENSE OF LIFE 35

4 A TAX *SOLUTION*? 49

5 WINNING THE IMMIGRATION WARS 69

6 HELPING FELLOW AMERICANS 85

7 EDUCATION THAT WORKS 103

8 COMMONSENSE LEGAL REFORM 117

9 DEVELOPING ENERGY RESOURCES 137

10 COUNTERING GLOBAL THREATS 159

11 FULL SPEED AHEAD 175

NOTES 183

INDEX 199

COMMON SENSE

I'S TIME FOR COMMON SENSE TO PREVAIL IN AMERICA.

This concept, you might say, is not rocket science. But it isn't trivial to pursue a course of political action based on such a simple and practical statement. You need a lot of motivation (and some common sense of your own) to undertake it.

There is a great dearth of common sense in this country today. Too many of the people who hold public office in the United States of America at the beginning of this twenty-first century have made a career of responding to special-interest groups or bowing to the latest public opinion polls. Under the pressure, their minds have turned off. Certain opinions have become well entrenched. They are resistant to ideas that threaten their way of thinking and operating.

They don't particularly think of themselves as lacking common sense, but neither does it come to their minds as a valuable quality to cultivate. They're distracted with the job at hand, which consists of running messy and complex organizations without getting shot out of the saddle. Some of them trumpet other special qualities: "I'm a risk-taker" or "I'm tough; I'm shrewd" or, conversely, "I care." But you hardly ever hear, "I have common sense." Maybe they think it sounds too...common.

I think that common sense has been underrated and underutilized. Consequently, we wobble and weave our way through life. Without it, we certainly can't expect to do a good job of leading other people over the long haul.

To have common sense, I believe a person needs to possess some pervasive qualities, including:

1. A good mind, one that can evaluate the contemporary state of affairs with logic and sound reason

2. A capacity to learn, both from personal experience and from the experience of others (including written history)

3. A dynamic balance between right and left, to and fro, black and white, yes and no

4. Self-confidence that is born from a measure of success in life, the kind of confidence that

humbly acknowledges the contributions of others

5. Flexibility, which enables ongoing innovation, self-evaluation, and course correction

6. Consistency and integrity—the hallmarks of trustworthiness

7. A kind of patience that comes from knowing when to make a wise move

8. An unflagging motivation to take hold of life

9. A generosity of spirit that looks for ways to serve others

Common sense tells us that we cannot function without other people. It enables us to balance self-preservation with self-sacrifice. It informs our discussions and even our heated arguments. It can make us capable of great feats. It undergirds our perseverance.

A public officeholder with common sense gets the job done, providing the most benefit to the largest number of people with the least wasted effort and money.

Lots of ordinary people have common sense, but they are frustrated—big-time—by the others around them who lack it. They wish that more of their leaders had the ability to think straight, to see the big picture, and to strategize wisely. They recognize that common sense is basic to successful living.

As you read this book, you will see clearly that common sense is the underlying theme. It could almost be the title. I take a commonsense approach to my own life, and that carries over into my public life.

Reviving the American Spirit: A Strategy of Hope for the 21st Century is a commonsense-guided tour of the big issues that confront us today in the United States of America. May you be the kind of reader whose own common sense makes you able to appreciate sound strategies when you see them.

CHAPTER 1

BLACK AND REPUBLICAN

GROWING UP IN DETROIT IN THE 1960S, MY BASIC BELIEF WAS THAT REPUBLICANS WERE THE ENEMY. EVERYONE TOLD ME THAT REPUBLICANS ARE UNCARING, SADISTIC, ONLY FOR THE RICH, EVEN EVIL INCARNATE. THAT'S THE WAY I CAME UP, AND THAT'S STILL THE ATTITUDE OF MANY AFRICAN AMERICANS TODAY. IT MAY BE A STEREOTYPE, BUT IT ALSO HAPPENS TO BE A REALITY.

Like probably 99 percent of the black kids of my era, my big hero was Martin Luther King Jr., along with the Democrats who had given him so much support in his fight for civil rights, John F. Kennedy and Bobby Kennedy. Because all the people around me thought Democrats were superior, it never occurred to me to question it. Until I went to college, I don't think I had ever met a Republican personally.

Not that everything a Democrat might do met with our approval. We all knew about corruption in high Democratic places. But our parents would vote for those candidates in the next election anyway, and so would we, when we were old enough to vote. The simple fact was that the Democrats could count on the black vote. That's still the case.

However—and this is big—a shift is beginning to take place. People are stopping to think about their political persuasion. They are taking a hard look at their opinions and their voting behavior. They are reconsidering their reflex to vote Democrat, and they are reconsidering their other reflex—to bash any Republican candidate around.

Guys like me are showing up on the scene. I'm a black Republican. A *what*? An African American man who is also a staunch Republican and who wants to represent a multiethnic constituency by serving in the United States Senate. A black guy who spends a lot of time thinking hard about the issues, who's a center-right conservative, and who talks about balance and common sense. Now that's radical.

New Territory

How did I get to this place?

In 1980, when I was twenty-four years old, the Republican Party held its convention in my city, Detroit. Ronald Reagan was nominated as their candidate for president of the United States. I happened to watch him on television. The man impressed me.

I had never known anyone who had done this, but I decided to read for myself the platform statements of both parties. Political party platforms are not your typical bedside reading. But once I got my hands on a copy of the text of that year's Republican Party platform, I was as enthralled as if I had a dramatic novel in my hands. What parts of the 1980 Republican Platform stood out to me?

The preamble of the platform statement minced no words about the state of the Democratic Party. After summarizing the muddled state of the United States economy and foreign affairs, the document stated:

> The Carter Administration is the unhappy and inevitable consequence of decades of increasingly outmoded Democratic domination of our national life. Over the past four years it has repeatedly demonstrated that it has no basic goals other than the perpetuation of its own rule and no guiding principle other than the fleeting insights provided by the latest opinion poll.[1]

You would think that I would have been put off by this kind of language. But I wasn't, especially not as I began to read about my own fellow black citizens and neighbors:

> For two generations, especially since the mid-1960s, the Democrats have deliberately perpetuated a status of federally subsidized poverty and manipulated dependency for millions of Americans. This is especially so for blacks and Hispanics, many of whom remain pawns of the bureaucracy, trapped outside the social and economic mainstream of American life.[2]

As I pressed on, I found out what the Republicans proposed to do about the problems in America, including issues that hit close to home for a native Detroiter:

> **Black Americans.** Our fundamental answer to the economic problems of black Americans is the same answer we make to all Americans—full employment without inflation through economic growth. First and foremost, we are committed to a policy of economic expansion through tax-rate reductions, spending restraint, regulatory reform, and other incentives. As the Party of Lincoln, we remain equally and steadfastly committed to the equality of rights for all citizens, regardless of race.
>
> **Abortion.** While we recognize the differing views on this question among Americans in general—and

in our own Party—we affirm our support of a constitutional amendment to restore protection of the right to life for unborn children.

Strong Families. The family is the foundation of our social order. It is the school of democracy. Its daily lessons—cooperation, tolerance, mutual concern, responsibility, industry—are fundamental to the order and progress of our Republic. But the Democrats have shunted the family aside. They have given its power to the bureaucracy, its jurisdiction to the courts, and its resources to government grantors....Unlike the Democrats, we do not advocate new federal bureaucracies with ominous power to shape a national family order. Rather, we insist that all domestic policies, from child care and schooling to Social Security and the tax code, must be formulated with the family in mind.[3]

I read the entire document, and then I read its counterpart, the Democratic Platform, which of course talked about the same issues. Without a doubt, the Republican Party stood best for what I believed.

What could I do with this information? Just quietly slip my vote to Ronald Reagan in the upcoming election? I thought deeply about the implications of my decision, and then I decided to launch out into uncharted territory.

I became a member of the Republican Party.

The Democratic Party Left Me

Like Ronald Reagan, who was also a "convert" from the Democratic Party to the GOP, I could say, "I didn't leave the Democratic Party. The Democratic Party left me." In speeches, he had repeated that declaration so many times that it was well known. His decision had come after the Democrats moved further to the left on social, economic, defense, and international issues. Their views had alienated him, they had alienated Middle America, and they had alienated me—a young African American man living in a city where almost 90 percent of the residents identified themselves as Democrats.

It shocked me to take such a hard look at what both parties actually stood for. Given what my value system was, it was a *revelation* for me to find that the Democrats, the party that I thought represented everything I accepted as true, were standing *opposite* to the core of what I really believed.

The Democrats were my real enemies, in terms of what they stood for. I was a young African American male with a wife and growing family, pastoring a storefront church in Motown.

And I was, as it turns out, also a *Republican.*

Dipping Into Black History

My newfound Republican identity may have been news to me, but it would not have been news to my forebears.

The Republican Party is called the "party of Lincoln."

And because Abraham Lincoln was the great emancipator of the slaves, my forefathers considered themselves Republicans. They voted for Republican candidates. They themselves ran for office as Republicans—and often won.

Unbelievable as that may seem to most of us today, blacks have not always cast their votes with the party of FDR and JFK. Quite the opposite. They voted for the candidates who represented the true civil rights party—the Republicans.

When the Democrats began to woo them with promises of a better future, many black citizens even got upset about it (more about this later). They remembered not only the Civil War but also the whole history of the Democratic Party.

The Democratic Party was founded in 1792 by Thomas Jefferson. In what is now confusing terminology, it was called the Democratic-Republican Party, and Jefferson was called a "Republican." The party later split into the Democratic Party and the Whig Party (defunct by the time of the Civil War, leaving just the Democratic Party to represent the party Jefferson founded). The Republican Party was a latecomer on the scene, formed in 1854 specifically for the purpose of opposing slavery in the new territories. Its early policies found their inspiration in those of the Whigs, and its early members came from the declining Whig Party, the Free Soil Party, and the American Party.

The Democrats were the ones who in 1820 had

passed the Missouri Compromise, which reversed a previous policy established in 1789 that had prohibited slavery in federal territories. The Democrat-controlled United States Congress had thereby authorized slavery in almost half of the federal territories, some of which subsequently became new states where slavery was permitted.

To justify this decision, the Democrats had to ignore the Declaration of Independence and other founding documents. One of the Founding Fathers, former President John Quincy Adams, wrote a letter to the 12th Congressional District in 1839 in which he stated:

> The first step of the slaveholder to justify by argument the peculiar institutions [of slavery] is to deny the self-evident truths of the Declaration of Independence. He denies that all men are created equal. He denies that they have inalienable rights.[4]

Building on the Missouri Compromise, the Democrats also passed a law in 1850 that required Northerners to return runaway slaves to their masters in the South. This Fugitive Slave Law became a thinly veiled excuse for slave-hunters to kidnap free blacks in the North and carry them into slavery in the South, denying them the constitutional benefit of habeas corpus and a fair jury trial. The Underground Railroad became the passage of last resort, taking slaves all the way to Canada and out of the reach of the Democrats' Fugitive Slave Law.

The Civil War was fought largely because of slavery. Any economic and states' rights issues that may be put forward as causes of the war are ultimately traceable to the institution of slavery. There was a clear difference between Republicans (mostly in the North) and Democrats (mostly in the South), especially where opinions about racial equality were concerned. The Southern Democrats pressed the issue to the breaking point, becoming willing to secede from the United States as a nation based on white supremacy. A lot of blood from both sides was spilled before the Rebels conceded.

North-South lines were blurred after the war. For a time during Reconstruction, many southern states became Republican instead of Democrat, and newly freed blacks, almost all of whom considered themselves Republicans for obvious reasons, found their way quickly into political office. This development was so swift and so unwelcome to the Democrats, most of whom had fought as Rebels, that they employed a variety of methods to regain power, including physical violence. In 1866, Democrats formed a group whose declared purpose was to break down Republican government and to enable Democrats to regain control. What was the name of this group? It was the Ku Klux Klan.

The Klan targeted Republicans in general, and terrorized whites as well as blacks.[5] This fact is irrefutably confirmed by testimony given before congressional committee in 1872[6] as well as by other documentation.[7]

This fact may come as quite a surprise to Republicans as well as Democrats. We have some national history to live down!

Getting Our History Straight

In actual fact, African American political history goes back over two centuries. It goes way back, well beyond W. E. B. Dubois, Martin Luther King Jr., Malcolm X, and others who have become prominent in the past hundred years or so.

The fact of the matter is that African American political history starts where all American political history starts—in 1787, when the United States Constitution was written.

There are people who will tell you that the Constitution is anti-black, because of the so-called Three-Fifths Clause. They will tell you that you can't trust a document that states that a black is only three-fifths of a person. What they do not realize is that the Three-Fifths Clause was inserted to equalize representation in Congress. The statement has nothing to do with the value of a person as an individual. In the new United States, each state was going to get one representative for each thirty thousand inhabitants. Some southern states had a disproportionate number of slave inhabitants, and, rather than allow them to have increased proslavery congressional power based on their slave-inflated population figures, the framers of the Constitution compromised; slave populations could be tallied at 60 percent (that is, three-fifths) in the calculations. Even the great black abolitionist Frederick Douglass came to understand that this was true. He wrote:

> [T]he Constitution is a glorious liberty document. Read its preamble; consider its purposes....Now, take the Constitution according to its plain reading and I defy the presentation of a single pro-slavery clause in it. On the other hand, it will be found to contain principles and purposes entirely hostile to the existence of slavery.[8]

Ratified in 1865, 1868, and 1870 respectively, the Thirteenth, Fourteenth, and Fifteenth Amendments were added to the Constitution to abolish slavery and to ensure the civil rights of blacks.

> ...No State shall make or enforce any law which shall abridge the privileges or immunities of citizens of the United States; nor shall any State deprive any person of life, liberty, or property, without due process of law; nor deny to any person within its jurisdiction the equal protection of the laws....
>
> —FROM THE FOURTEENTH AMENDMENT
> TO THE U.S. CONSTITUTION

Interestingly, when the Fourteenth Amendment came to a vote, it is a matter of record that not one Democrat in either the House or the Senate voted for it.[9]

Making a New Deal

Fast-forward to the twentieth century. From the time of the Reconstruction after the Civil War until the Great Depression, the Republican Party dominated United States political affairs, benefiting from the association of the Democratic Party with the Confederacy. Competition was fierce, and the Democrats took a turn at the helm in the 1880s and 1890s when Grover Cleveland was president for two terms, and again in the teens and into the 1920s, when Woodrow Wilson was president. Southern states, led by Democrats, circumvented the federal civil rights protections of the constitutional amendments by implementing poll taxes, segregated schools and public places, restrictive "Jim Crow" laws, and dozens of other political tactics.

After the crash of the stock market and the ensuing Great Depression, the political power was handed over decisively to a Democrat, Franklin Delano Roosevelt, in 1932. Part of his election strategy was a subtle appeal to blacks, from whom he stood to gain more votes than he would lose, an appeal based on ongoing events that included lynchings perpetrated by white southern Democrats.[10] African Americans also switched to the Democratic Party because they saw Roosevelt as the disburser of federal wealth through New Deal programs. Roosevelt is known for his New Deal coalition of special interest groups that included labor unions, liberals, African Americans, and southern whites.

12

Journalist Theodore H. White, famous for his series The Making of a President, wrote in a 1956 article in *Collier's* magazine:

> Years ago, to be sure, the Negroes, still wedded to the memory of Abraham Lincoln, were...solidly Republican and regarded the Democrats among themselves as freaks. ("I remember," says Roy Wilkins, executive secretary of the National Association for the Advancement of Colored People, "when I was young in Kansas City, the kids threw rocks at Negroes on our street who dared vote Democratic.") But Franklin D. Roosevelt changed all that; his New Deal was aimed directly at Americans in distress, and distress has been house companion of the Negroes since their history began. With Roosevelt, government came to mean Social Security, relief ("Let Jesus lead me and welfare feed me," was a depression chant of the Negroes), unemployment compensation, housing, strong unions open to Negro membership. In overwhelming, earthquake proportions, the Negro vote became Democratic in 1936 and 1940.[11]

Subsequent to this, both parties could claim a record of civil rights victories as well as failures. Democrat Harry Truman alienated many by his energetic efforts on behalf of protection for African American rights. Civil rights legislation, which included a proposed Civil Rights Commission, was voted down by members of his own party.[12] Republican Dwight Eisenhower instituted a number of civil rights reforms in areas that were under his direct oversight, such as the federal government and the District of Columbia. Many of his other efforts ended with setbacks, usually because of the legislative process. But more than 60 percent of black voters had chosen to vote for him, strongly influenced by the endorsement of African American Congressman Adam Clayton Powell Jr.[13]

The unity between the two of the original New Deal groups began to fall apart over civil rights issues, with many southern whites, who favored segregation, giving their support to Republicans in 1964. The southern blacks and their northern counterparts, who had long since become established in industrialized states such as my own, Michigan, retrenched in the Democratic Party, a position that was reinforced greatly as John F. Kennedy showed his overt support for desegregation. He championed the Civil Rights Act (conceived during the Eisenhower administration), which was signed into law by Lyndon Johnson after JFK was assassinated.

Notably, although the Civil Rights Act was finalized by a Democratic executive, it was only because of Republicans in Congress that it was voted into law. Democrats held a two-thirds majority in both houses, and southern Democrats in the Senate mounted a filibuster. In the end, only a total of 198 Democrats (out of 315) cast their votes for the Civil Rights Act.[14] The Act was passed only because of the overwhelming support of the Republicans.

Nevertheless, right up to the present time, the black vote in the United States has stayed solidly in the Democrats' column. And yet, as I said already, that is beginning to shift back to the way it used to be.

So much of this history has been hushed up. I'm presenting it in this chapter for you to read and understand. You can look up the documentation yourself.

Because I have my own sights on a seat in the "100 Club"—the United States Senate—I find another historical fact particularly interesting, namely, that the first three black United States Senators were all Republicans. They were the Rev. Hiram R. Revels of Georgia (1870–1871), Blanche K. Bruce of Mississippi (1875–1881), and the Rev. Edward Brooke of Massachusetts (1967–1979). The first-ever black Democrat to become a U.S. senator was Carol Moseley-Braun of Illinois (1993–1999), and she has been followed by a second, Barack Obama, also from Illinois, in 2005. It's time to bring back some balance; the Senate needs a black Republican senator.

Educated to Serve

None of this was made known to me as I was growing up in Detroit.

A 1973 graduate of Henry Ford High School in Detroit, I married Deborah, and we attended and graduated from the same Oklahoma Bible college. Together, we planted a church in the city of Detroit, and I also earned an associate's degree from nearby Oakland Community College. As we began to raise our family, I wanted more education, so I split my time between my family, my church, political work, and the University of Michigan, which had a campus within driving distance. By 1987, I had another degree, this one in sociology, psychology, and history.

Over the next few years, I continued to pastor my growing congregation and to think about the issues that affected their lives and mine. My church was growing fast. I had started it with sixty people in a storefront in 1979 when I was twenty-three years old, freshly graduated from Bible school.

From the beginning, I understood the people I served. I had had a rough time growing up, but I had gotten myself straightened out. I had always held a job of some sort since I was fourteen years old. Before that, I had worked with my father, who owned a construction and landscaping company. I had learned to manage a lot at one time—job, school, and so forth. I was going to need that ability.

After a short time, our church moved to a borrowed room in a recreation center, and then we obtained our own storefront. In a city full of storefront churches, there was no guarantee that ours would stand out. But it did.

It outgrew every facility. Eventually, we moved out of the city itself into the suburb of Southfield, where we established a headquarters campus on 110 acres of land. Today, the church is still growing. We have well over 21,000 members, satellite churches in many other cities, a school, and a flourishing outreach to the disadvantaged. Unquestionably, Word of Faith is the largest church in the entire state of Michigan.

As the years went by, I began to realize that both my mind and my heart were telling me the same thing: as one who was primarily a servant of the people, I wanted to run for public office myself.

As a Republican.

CHAPTER 2

THE MORALITY CONNECTION

EVEN THOUGH I WAS KNOWN TO BE A REPUBLICAN, AND DETROIT WAS 88 PERCENT DEMOCRAT, IN 1989 I DECIDED TO RUN FOR AN AT-LARGE SEAT ON THE DETROIT CITY COUNCIL. FORTY-THREE PERCENT (105,000) OF DETROIT RESIDENTS CAST THEIR VOTES FOR ME, AND I BECAME THE FIRST KNOWN REPUBLICAN TO HAVE BEEN ELECTED TO DETROIT CITY COUNCIL SINCE BEFORE WORLD WAR II.

I am proud of the fact that (unlike the present Detroit city government) our council balanced the city budget while meeting the needs of our constituents.

Such economic successes, however, would not have provided adequate motivation for my continued interest in public service. I served my full four-year term, and I remained active in Republican affairs on the state and national level after I left that post.

Then, like my fellow Detroiter, U.S. Senator Carl Levin, I decided to make the jump from the local office of city councilperson to the national one of United States Senator. The primary reason I decided to run against the Democratic incumbent who will be my opponent in the 2006 Senate race is my opposition to her ultraliberal stand on issues such as the protection of life, traditional marriage, and national security. She voted against the federal same-sex marriage ban in 2004, against the marriage penalty relief in President Bush's tax cut proposal, against increasing funds for national defense after 9/11, and in favor of cuts to intelligence funding.

In other words, my primary motivation for deciding to run for the United States Senate is both a moral and a social one. I want to be able to serve more people than I can do at the present time, to serve as a voice for the people of Michigan in a place where vital decisions are made.

Moral Integrity

We talk about the issues as if they have no overlap with each other, but they do. For example, economic policy affects education. Education affects jobs. Jobs affect the tax base, which in turn affects public education. Tax policy and environmental standards affect international trade. And in these days of terrorism threats, almost any issue relates to national security. All of the issues are interrelated. Government cannot be compartmentalized any better than daily life can, and no single issue can dominate the discussion for too long without consideration for other issues.

A good leader will actively work to keep public policy on the right track in all of the areas where he or she has oversight, provoking discussion and instigating change wherever necessary to achieve valid goals, always keeping the big picture in mind. The lives of the best leaders prove to be seamless in their public and private aspects.

Another word for this is *integrity.* By definition, integrity implies that "what you see is what you get." Such leaders don't have anything to hide. If people who run for political office have stable and successful private lives, you can expect that to carry through into their public lives. They may not be 100 percent perfect, and they may not root for the same football team as you do, but you can be sure that they will be honest and competent and energetic in their efforts to use their leadership gifts for the common good.

A candidate who is morally pure has a clear conscience. No ugly secrets lurk beneath the surface. The person will be the same in public as he is in private. He or she can be trusted.

Good Morals Create Good Government

You can take this idea even further. I am a strong proponent of the idea that good morals create good government. In fact, I believe that there's no such thing as "good government" without a moral basis to it.

Most of the verification for this statement, unfortunately, is negative. We see it all around us. When the moral quality of those in governmental positions is off-track, damage results.

Case in point: Things are off-track when politicians campaign on the basis of allowing more and more license for what used to be recognized as perversion. Things are off-track when you need police protection in public schools and when half of the married couples in the nation (and your neighborhood) are divorced. Things are off-track when every year more than a million babies are aborted in a country that was founded on the basis of life, liberty, and equality for all human beings.

The principle applies as well to a family or a business as it does to a unit of government. Where moral principles are the basis for action, good results follow—thriving stable growth and cooperation that provide the best for all of the people. Good ideas are brought to fulfillment by good management. The overall conditions of the society improve.

There's a scriptural proverb that expresses it well: "When the righteous are in authority, the people rejoice; but when the wicked rule, the people groan."[1] But the "righteous" (those who hold to strong moral principles) must step forward to shoulder this authority, and, in our representative form of government, the people must recognize their responsibility to vote them in.

You can't legislate morality (although you can create a framework that supports morality), but you can legislate *morally.* You can legislate with integrity and a clear conscience. You can legislate with the goal of serving the good of the people who elected you. You don't have to be religious to be moral. To a large extent, all you need is common sense.

Common sense told the people who stood against slavery that the slaves were human beings just as they were. They looked and they said, "This guy looks like me. He breathes the same air as me. He has eyes, nose, mouth—same as I do. If I teach this guy how to read, he can do anything I do. He can learn the same as I learn."

In the same way, common sense should tell us that we're dealing with babies, little human beings, not pieces of protoplasm. If you have ever seen a picture of a fetus, you know for a fact that he's just like you, only tiny. Once you looked like that yourself.

God was legislated out of American public schools in the early 1960s, and the results have been harmful by anyone's standards. For nearly 180 years, a simple prayer had been prayed by public schoolchildren: "Almighty God, we acknowledge our dependence upon Thee and we beg Thy blessing upon us, our parents, our teachers, and our country." But in 1962–1963, that prayer was ruled illegal.[2] It's hard to miss the aftereffects—teen pregnancy soared more than 400 percent, divorce went up over 120 percent, and SAT scores declined for eighteen years straight.

Now I know as well as you do that the cause and effect is not quite as simple as that. But you can't ignore the connection. There is one. When morals slip in government, they slip in society. And everyone suffers.

The consequences are like a giant mop-up operation that never ends. Civil authorities spend all their efforts playing catch-up and patch-up, but the slippage just accelerates. To change the metaphor, it's like a leak in the dike or a breach in the levee. What started as a small failing of "structural integrity" becomes, under pressure, a devastating flood.

Can such a thing be reversed? Or should we all pack up our families and flee to somewhere far away from voting precincts and ubiquitous news broadcasts?

I believe—and I'm glad I'm not alone in this—that there is still time to reverse the downward trend.

Faith of Our Fathers

People have forgotten that our nation was founded on a moral basis and that it was a Christian one, for the most part.

If you ask average Americans why the colonies fought to become independent of Great Britain, most will repeat what they remember learning in school, which is something about "taxation without representation." Well, that was one reason—out of twenty-seven—but it was certainly not the only reason. In the Declaration of Independence, it was listed in the seventeenth place. (It does happen to be the shortest sentence in the list and is perhaps therefore more memorable.) However, the larger number of the twenty-seven reasons given for separation from Great Britain had to do with moral rectitude, fairness in governing colonial affairs, aggression and coercion, and the compromise of public safety.

Slavery is a moral issue. King George III was pro-slavery, and the British Empire practiced slavery. Some of the colonies had tried to pass antislavery legislation, but the king had vetoed it. This kind of overbearing injustice exasperated the colonial leaders. Their spokesman, Thomas Jefferson, penned the immortal declaration: "We hold these truths to be self-evident, that all men are created equal, that they are endowed by their Creator with certain unalienable Rights, that among these are Life, Liberty and the pursuit of Happiness."[3] In the Declaration of Independence, he summarized what amounts to a commonsense approach to tyranny, the twenty-seven grievances against the Crown that transgress the "self-evident" truths of human life.

Jefferson and his colleagues derived their ideals about the pursuit of individual liberty from John Locke, from European philosophers, and from the Bible. Thomas Jefferson is known to have been one of the least religious of the Founding Fathers. However, he does not hedge as he concludes the document: "We, therefore, the Representatives of the united States of America, in General Congress, Assembled, appealing to the Supreme Judge of the world for the rectitude of our intentions...."[4] He and the colonial assembly appealed to God, and today we should not be afraid of doing the same.

So it is patently disingenuous to claim that—merely for economic reasons—the Founding Fathers provoked the Revolutionary War and gave their lives to establishing a viable alternative to British rule. Not all of them were Christians, and some of them were slaveholders themselves, yet their operating principles were heavily informed by Christian morality; they knew clearly that the fledgling nation needed a strong moral foundation to survive. John Adams, in a letter to Thomas Jefferson many years after the establishment of the new nation, spoke for dozens of other founding leaders when he wrote:

> The general principles on which the fathers achieved independence were...the general principles of Christianity....Now I will avow what I then believed, and now believe, that those general principles of Christianity are as eternal and immutable as the existence and attributes of God.[5]

This is not to say that the Founding Fathers wanted to limit the definition of these principles only to Christianity. On the contrary, they embraced a wide variety of religious expression, including Jews and Muslims. One of them, Dr. Benjamin Rush, wrote:

> Such is my veneration for every religion that reveals the attributes of the Deity... that I had rather see the opinions of Confucius or Mohamed inculcated upon our youth than see them grow up wholly devoid of a system of religious principles.[6]

Jefferson recommended that the new Great Seal of the United States should depict the biblical story of the children of Israel in the wilderness, led by a cloud by day and a pillar of fire by night, and that the national motto should include God's name. Benjamin Franklin, who also served on the first committee to design the Great Seal, recommended that the Seal depict:

> Moses standing on the Shore, and extending his Hand over the Sea, thereby causing the same to over-whelm Pharaoh who is sitting in an open Chariot, a Crown on his Head and a Sword in his Hand. Rays from a Pillar of Fire in the Clouds reaching to Moses, to express that he acts by Command of the Deity.[7]

The official translation of the U.S. State Department for the Latin phrase *Annuit Cœptis*, which appears on the Great Seal of the United States above the image of the eye of [God's] Providence, is "He (God) has favored our undertakings."[8]

It is my firm conviction, based on the history of our nation, that the principles invoked by the Founding

Fathers have been uniquely successful in establishing the United States of America as a premier nation. The moral principles they invoked are foundational both to good laws and to wise administration.

The "father of our country," George Washington, did not shy away from giving credit to these foundational principles. In his Farewell Address of 1796, he asserted:

> Of all the dispositions and habits which lead to political prosperity, religion and morality are indispensable supports.[9]

The So-Called "Wall of Separation Between Church and State"

People have been brainwashed to the extent that they believe government and morality (often limited to "religion") are polar opposites. I run into this all the time as a Republican who is running for public office and who also happens to be a Christian minister. When I give a speech, even fellow Republicans come up to me and say, "Isn't it illegal for you, a minister, to run for public office?"

No, it is not any more illegal for me to run for public office than it is for any citizen to do so. It is also not illegal for me to talk about morality in the same breath.

I can hear the rejoinder: "Well, the Bill of Rights says that there's a wall of separation between church and state...doesn't it?"

No, that's not what the Bill of Rights says. And you

would be surprised at what the so-called "wall" was meant to accomplish. Let's dip into a little more history.

Church and State 101

First of all, let's review the wording of the First Amendment to the Constitution. The amendment was added in 1789, and it reads, "Congress shall make no law establishing religion or prohibiting the free exercise thereof." That's it. That's the whole thing. It was intended quite simply to keep the federal government from establishing a state church or denomination, while at the same time encouraging the "free exercise" of religious principles throughout society.

The phrase that we know as the Establishment Clause, "wall of separation between church and state," is found in a letter that Thomas Jefferson wrote in 1802 to the Danbury Baptist Association in Connecticut. The Danbury Baptists were a religious minority in their state, and they were worried that the government would misuse legislative language to control the free exercise of their religious rights. So they wrote a letter to Jefferson to get his opinion on the matter.

In his reply, the body of which is 290 words long, appears a phrase of seven words, "wall of separation between church and state":

> ...Believing with you that religion is a matter which lies solely between man & his god, that he owes

account to none other for his faith or his worship, that the legitimate powers of government reach actions only, and not opinions, I contemplate with sovereign reverence that act of the whole American people which declared that their legislature should make no law respecting an establishment of religion, or prohibiting the free exercise thereof, thus building a wall of separation between church and state... [10]

For the first 170 years after the letter was written, it was used to buttress opinions that matched those of the man who wrote it. It was understood to have been written to reassure the Danbury Baptists—and, by extension, any church body—that the First Amendment to the United States Constitution guarantees freedom from government interference in expressions of worship, including public ones. Over that period of time, occasional court decisions quoted from the letter (quoting more than the seven words we know best today). [11] They quoted it to underscore the idea that the government has no business legislating worship.

However, in 1947, the Supreme Court (a court that had been packed by FDR with Democrats, by the way) changed the meaning of the phrase by taking it out of context in writing their decision in *Everson v. Board of Education.* Their decision did not even mention that their predecessors had used Jefferson's letter for the opposite reason—to preserve the expression of religious values in society, not to prohibit them.

Next, in 1962, the Supreme Court went a step further, by defining "church" to mean any public religious activity, rather than only a formal religious denomination, and, without any precedent, by ruling that prayers in public schools were unconstitutional.[12] The slope was now very slippery. A profusion of ill-conceived decisions followed.

In 1954, for instance, in the Senate, liberal Democrats attached a rider to the IRS bill that made it illegal for nonprofit organizations to speak about political affairs. Since then, the pulpit has become the least free place in America in terms of speech. I believe that's flat-out wrong. A labor leader can stand up and say, "This candidate stands for what we believe in, and he's the one we're going to support." A homosexual activist or an environmentalist or a person from any other segment of society can do the same. But not a Christian minister. I believe that's a clear abridgment of First Amendment rights. It's never been tested in front of the Supreme Court, but I believe it's an infringement of the rights of a vast majority of Americans, and I'd like to do something about it.

Interestingly, the late Chief Justice William Rehnquist was very clear on the subject of the separation of church and state. In the 1985 case *Wallace v. Jaffree,* he wrote that the faulty focus on that phrase has triggered a...

> ...mischievous diversion of judges from the actual intentions of the drafters of the Bill of Rights...The

"wall of separation between church and state" is a metaphor based on bad history, a metaphor which has proved useless as a guide to judging. It should be frankly and explicitly abandoned.[13]

The purpose of the First Amendment was to keep government out of religion, not to keep religion out of government.

So it has become a complete misnomer. Remember that the next time the subject comes up. And you can be certain that it will come up.

Moral Values

As I engage in the political process, I will persist in contending for moral values, because I believe they represent the most good for those who are governed. I have no interest in turning the political arena into a church. I respect the fact that the governments of cities, states, and nations have distinct functions.

Yet my neighbor deserves to be served with the same level of integrity as my family or my congregation, and I will strive to administer any and all leadership roles from the identical moral foundation.

Government can only do so much. Even in the best of times, legislation informed by morality is only as good as the moral fiber of the people. Morality cannot be instituted by fiat. The second president of the United States, John Adams, uttered these words in a speech to a military gathering in 1798:

> [W]e have no government armed with power capable of contending with human passions unbridled by morality and religion.... Our Constitution was made only for a moral and religious people. It is wholly inadequate to the government of any other.[14]

The Constitution is a good document, but it's only a document. The business of governing belongs to people, different people in every generation. It is undeniably important to have a good, morally based constitution, but that piece of paper will not make much difference if a corrupt populace has elected corrupt leaders.

At the same time, we should realize that the Constitution of the United States, as it was written, has *worked*. It has provided a strong and solid framework for the development of the most prosperous and creative nation that the world has ever seen. I believe that it is sacrosanct and that it should not be changed or tinkered with except under the most dire circumstance.

You know the line, "If it ain't broke, don't fix it." The Constitution has held up remarkably well. It isn't faulty—although our interpretation of it can be. I believe we should study it to understand how it applies to the governmental complexities of today instead of revising it to suit our godless approach to instituted authority. And I believe we should elect honorable leaders who will make it their business to exercise their authority wisely.

CHAPTER 3

IN DEFENSE OF LIFE

SINCE THE 1973 SUPREME COURT *ROE V. WADE* DE-CISION, MORE THAN 45 MILLION ABORTIONS HAVE TAKEN PLACE IN THE UNITED STATES OF AMERICA, ACCORDING TO THE CENTERS FOR DISEASE CONTROL AND PREVENTON AND THE ALAN GUTTMACHER INSTITUTE.[1] THAT'S AN AVERAGE OF 4,000 ABORTIONS OCCURRING EVERY DAY.

What does 45 million look like? Imagine for a moment that the entire nation of Canada (which has almost 35 million inhabitants[2]) suffers a massive catastrophe. All of the people are killed. The empty windows of the tall buildings of Montreal, Toronto, and Vancouver become roosting places for birds. Schools and colleges, sports stadiums and provincial parks, highways and parking lots are eerily silent. Imagine that Michigan, my home state (currently inhabited by a little over 10 million citizens[3]), is included in the catastrophic depopulation of Canada. The seagulls soar all day and never see even a single tanker on Lake Huron or an SUV crossing the Mackinac Bridge. There is a news blackout about the calamity because there are no reporters left in all of Canada or Michigan—no newscasters and no public services. Picture that whole sweep of territory from the Pacific Ocean to the Atlantic, including the Great Lakes State, as a wilderness with no remaining human civilization in it. Even the descendants of the original native population are missing.

That's what the absence of 45 million people would look like.

That same number of people—45 million—has been put to death legally in our country in the past three and a half decades.

One group of nine justices who composed one Supreme Court in 1973 made their nation-altering decision despite the foundational affirmation of the Declaration of Independence, namely, "We hold these truths to be self-evident, that all men are created equal, that they are endowed by their Creator with certain un-alienable Rights, that among these are Life, Liberty and the pursuit of Happiness." What's the first right? The first right is the right to life, which is the right to *live.*

Abortion wasn't first invented in 1973, of course.

But that marks the year when the Supreme Court transferred the burden of guilt for the murder of innocent children to the head and shoulders of the government itself, making abortion the signature and hideous national sin of our time. In the years since then, whom may we have killed? What future scientists must we have cut down? What potential leaders have we sent to their graves before they were born? What ordinary, decent citizens have we determined did not deserve to live, people whose only liability was that they were inconveniently conceived somewhere in a state that lies within our borders? On what excuse were they destroyed? That abortion is a woman's "legal right" and "free choice."

Ninety-seven percent of all abortions have nothing to do with rape, incest, or protection of the life of the mother. That's where the arguments always go, in the effort to beat back those of us who are pro-life. Ninety-seven percent of all abortions take place because we don't consider the worth of individuals. We don't value people's lives. Neither do we realize that they are a national resource.

Economic Consequences of Abortion

Moral issues have economic consequences on a national level. Obviously, the first way to talk about abortion is in terms of the value of human life. But let's look at abortion in terms of the economics.

Think about it: if those more than 40 million people

who have lost their lives to abortion were alive, by now more than 15 million of them would be of working age. As we speak, they would be holding down—and creating—jobs. They would be consumers. Farmers and ranchers would be working to feed them. Builders would be constructing homes for them. Auto companies would be selling cars to them. They would be entrepreneurs and schoolteachers and office workers. They would be productive citizens of the United States.

Abortion statistics tell only part of the story. By now, a good number of those missing 45 million people would have married. They would be having children of their own. We can estimate that, conservatively, an additional 5 million young citizens of varying ages would be going to school, learning trades, developing social networks, requiring products and services, and contributing to the overall well-being of the nation.

Do you know what else these millions of citizens would be doing? They would be paying local, state, and federal taxes. They would be contributing to Social Security—up to $44 billion a year!

It's common knowledge that part of the problem with the Social Security system is our baby-boom population. As this post–World War II generation starts to retire, and as they prove to outlive their predecessors by many years on the average, the payment of obligatory Social Security benefits will skyrocket. But because the baby boom was followed by a "baby bust," we will have fewer employees—just when we need more—to pay into the Social Security system. Abortion is a significant factor in the lower, "bust" numbers over the past thirty years.

Social Security is a pay-as-you-go system. Your benefits do not come from a giant federal interest-accruing savings account in Washington. Your retirement benefits will come pretty much from the pockets of those who are currently in the workforce when you stop working. And the situation is now approaching a crisis point. You do not have to be informed about every nuance of the argument about Social Security to recognize that the crisis with which we now grapple would not even exist if the United States had not systematically eliminated millions of its own citizens.

When I mention this economic cost of abortion, people are dumbfounded. "What are you talking about? Say that again." These ramifications have never occurred to them before. I have spoken to nonreligious groups and libertarian groups, who, of course, are pro-choice and who do not expect to find any points of agreement with me. When I lay that down, they have to agree with it.

This is simple logic, basic common sense.

What is it that makes us think that we should allow legal abortion to continue? Shall we sigh deeply and shake our heads and give up the fight?

Not on your life.

Pre-Abortion-Rights History

The argument that is used in favor of abortion is the same one that used to be articulated in support of slavery. In 1857, a Democratic-controlled Supreme Court rendered the infamous *Dred Scott* decision, which stated that blacks were not human and therefore could be bought and sold as cattle. Their statement declared that slaves "had no rights which the white man was bound to respect; and that the Negro might justly and lawfully be reduced to slavery for his benefit."[4] The individual states were offered a choice as to whether or not to allow slavery. The argument that slaveholders used at the time was, "I have a right to do with my property what I want." "I have a choice." "On my own plantation, I can do whatever I want." Does that sound a little familiar?

It is worth noting that the people who advocated against that choice, the abolitionists, were largely Christians. From a moral point of view and according to their understanding of biblical truth, they believed that every man was fully human and should never be owned by another man. In order to stop slavery from spreading, some of them banded together to found the Republican Party. It was a challenging and confrontational time in history.

The new Republican Party nominated a man from Illinois as their candidate for president of the United States, Abraham Lincoln. He was not elected in a landslide. In fact, he only got 40 percent of the popular vote. His moral/religious platform offended a lot of people.

The Republican platform that year, 1860, contained such inflammatory language that I'm surprised it didn't go up in smoke. Points seven, eight, and nine read:[5]

7. That the new dogma, that the Constitution, of its own force, carries Slavery into any or all of the Territories of the United States, is a dangerous political heresy, at variance with the explicit provisions of that instrument itself, with contemporaneous exposition, and with legislative and judicial precedent; is revolutionary in its tendency, and subversive of the peace and harmony of the country.

8. That the normal condition of all the territory of the United States is that of freedom; That as our Republican fathers, when they had abolished Slavery in all our national territory, ordained that "no person should be deprived of life, liberty, or property, without due process of law," it becomes our duty, by legislation, whenever such legislation is necessary, to maintain this provision of the Constitution against all attempts to violate it; and we deny the authority of Congress, of a territorial legislature, or of any individuals, to give legal existence to Slavery in any Territory of the United States.

9.   That we brand the recent re-opening of the African slave-trade, under the cover of our national flag, aided by perversions of judicial power, as a crime against humanity and a burning shame to our country and age; and we call upon Congress to take prompt and efficient measures for the total and final suppression of that execrable traffic.

Those are fighting words, and the party of Lincoln carried through with their firm resolve to correct the wrongful institution of slavery in the United States of America, to reunite the Union, and to create a legacy for those of us who have followed.

It seems clear to me that *Roe v. Wade* is an equally criminal violation of the intent of the Founding Fathers. They are probably spinning in their graves to see that people have used the Constitution they wrote in the eighteenth century as a pretext for killing babies in the twentieth and twenty-first centuries. Legalized abortion deprives unborn children of their basic human rights just as slavery denied basic human rights to black slaves in the southern states before the Civil War. In choosing abortion, a mother is claiming superior rights over her child's right to live, just as slave owners were claiming superior rights over their slaves' right to freedom.

I'll say it again: the right to live is the biggest issue of all the issues in the United States today.

Traditional Families

I believe that the second-biggest issue is the protection of the traditional American family. Families didn't used to need protection. But in recent times, the word *family* has been redefined and mangled beyond recognition.

I believe that the nuclear family—defined as two parents and their children—is the fundamental building block of a healthy and stable society. My liberal opponent in the Senate race has been endorsed by and supports the gay rights movement. I'm on the other side of that divide. Where I come from, a family has a male daddy and a female mommy. Even those who live in single-parent homes are not mixed up about how parents are supposed to be defined. I don't "hate the sinner," but I truly deplore the insistence that "anything goes."

This strong viewpoint does not endear me to certain individuals, who are quick to label people like me "rigid," "intolerant," or even "bigoted." But this kind of reaction doesn't surprise me. By taking a stand for moral values issues, I've stepped into a snake pit.

I believe this fight is worth sustained effort. I feel that I owe it to the people I serve who are trying to hold the line in their homes and workplaces against Hollywood and the liberal Left media who make a lot of noise and who seem to have the upper hand. They don't recognize the fact that, in household after household, the prevailing values are traditional ones.

Making a Difference

When the Massachusetts Supreme Court decided in 2004 to legalize gay marriage (bypassing the established law-making process that involves elected legislators who serve the will of the people), citizens of many other states were justifiably alarmed. In a rush, eleven states put gay marriage bans on their ballots, and every one of them passed. Michigan is one of those states. These bans are a defensive measure because of the times we live in. They represent, at the same time, a positive statement about traditional marriage.

We cannot allow the judiciary, the "talking heads," and the left-wingers in academia to promulgate laws that violate our consciences. Their influence is out of proportion. They are far more secular than most of the people in the average community. Who gave them so much power? What allows them to overrule my vote and to make binding decisions that undermine what I stand for? How am I going to respond when I see the values of the American people being misrepresented?

As a citizen, I am going to exercise my voice and my vote to make sure that traditional family values remain at the heart of public policy. As a candidate and potential legislator, I am going to respond in practical ways with commonsense strategies that reinforce traditional standards and endorse family-friendly laws. For example:

Economic values

I favor a drastic revision of the tax code in this country. (You can read more about it in the next chapter.) Where families are concerned, I would take less money away from the average, hardworking American family. In the 1950s, the average household paid about 2 percent in federal income taxes. Today, the average is up to 27 percent—which is about the same as the percentage of the average family income that is provided by the wife's second income. Because of this tax burden, families cannot get ahead.

Family assistance

One of the hallmarks of my public life has been helping families in need. I strongly favor faith-based assistance programs that help individuals and families. They provide more than just handouts. Some of these programs help with abstinence-based sex education for youth, parenting programs, after-school programs, and domestic crisis programs. Some of them work to improve the economic health of families in poor neighborhoods. Faith-based assistance programs work.

Community values and education

I believe that moral and ethical problems can be best solved at home within families and their local communities (with help from local organizations when needed). For instance, I don't feel that the government should be limiting your freedom to educate your children. If you want to send your child to a private school, you should be able to do so. One of your reasons for preferring a private school—assuming you can afford it, which links back to the economic and tax issues—may be so that you can avoid some of the government-mandated components of a public school education such as sex education with an overtly liberal bias.

The appeal of common sense

Commonsense solutions are straightforward. They call a spade a spade, not a diversified shovel. Yes, they recognize that the American population is not homogeneous. However, a commonsense approach is fair to those who do not share my set of values, without providing inordinate rewards for them.

A commonsense approach keeps federal fingers off the local family. Is Congress the most reasonable source for fair determinations about the welfare of my family? That's a rhetorical question. I do not buy into the top-down approach to solving societal problems across the country. I strongly believe that a strong America is built one family at a time and that any threats to the welfare of ordinary families should be resisted.

African American Families

One real obvious way in which African Americans line up with the moral principles of the Republican Party is their support, which is almost unanimous, for traditional marriage—one man and one woman.

Heterosexual marriage is part of the bedrock of black culture.

The issues I stand for—traditional family values, pro-life, and the like—have been pivotal for many African Americans in recent elections, and they have caused many African Americans to switch from the Democratic Party to the Republican. With their ears, they hear a message of "diversity" from the Democratic Party, but with their eyes, they see intolerance for the unsung citizens, black or white or any color, who happen to hold to traditional values. Where conservative values are concerned, the African American community is generally more conservative than the Republican Party.

I belong to a coalition of African American leaders who approved and signed a document called the Black Contract with America on Moral Values that was released to the public in February of 2005. This contract, which focuses on issues of righteousness and justice, begins with a section on "family reconstruction" in which abortion is deplored and traditional marriage is recognized as an endangered institution worthy of protection. This contract, developed by the High Impact Leadership Coalition, is a petition-style document that urges people to support lawmakers who will enact policies that promote its goals, specifically to "improve the plight of black America."[6] The document was inspired by the 1994 Republican Contract with America, which was one of the achievements of Newt Gingrich and other conservatives. The original Contract with America set forth goals and made promises that were conditional upon the outcome of elections and the signers' ongoing efforts. Similarly, those of us who have signed the Black Contract with America on Moral Values pledge to do all that is within our power to restore and reestablish traditional moral values. This is no small task in a world where fundamental life standards have been decimated in the culture war.

I'm going to continue to push hard against the ultra-liberal drift of our nation's legislative policies. I believe that the majority of the citizens of this country desire and deserve to be represented by legislators like me, people who will not be hesitant to stand, as Abraham Lincoln said, "with firmness in the right, as God gives us to see the right."

CHAPTER 4

A Tax *SOLUTION*?

Y OU KNOW THE OLD LINE ABOUT NOTHING BEING
UNIVERSALLY CERTAIN EXCEPT DEATH—AND TAXES.
BUT THE SAYING DOESN'T SPECIFY WHAT *KIND* OF TAXES.
(NOR DOES IT TELL US...MIGHT THAT MEAN DEATH *BY*
TAXATION?)

Nobody likes the subject. We hate to pay taxes, and
talking about them isn't very popular either. But we
need to do both. And, if possible, we need to reform the
system so that it is less painful for everyone. The health
of our economy and our well-being as citizens depend
on having a workable system of taxation.

In brief, I believe that both labor and capital should
be liberated from high taxes (and bureaucratic tax

forms) and that free enterprise is the best tool for the economic growth of a nation. High taxes burden the economy. They put too high a price on the productivity, labor, innovation, and capital formation of the nation's citizens.

No government in history has been able to better do for its citizens what they could do for themselves if they were allowed to follow their instincts and aspirations. It stands to reason that to the degree that you liberate the American taxpayer, to that degree will you unshackle your economy. If we make it possible for people to keep more of what they earn, they will have the incentive to earn more, which in turn creates more than adequate tax revenues.

The Tax Dragon

Some of the leaders I admire the most have already wrestled the tax dragon to the mat, which convinced me that further progress is achievable. One of them, Jack Kemp, helped to prove the theory that lower taxes result in higher federal revenues. Remember the Kemp-Roth Tax Act of 1981 (officially known as the Economic Recovery Tax Act, or ERTA)—which resulted in the greatest burst of national prosperity in two decades? Kemp-Roth reduced the marginal income tax rates so that the top rate went down to 50 percent (from 70 percent) and the bottom rate went down to 11 percent (from 14 percent), with the rates indexed for inflation. The purpose of the tax reductions was to encourage economic growth and to give incentives for business development and savings.

Lowering taxes may seem to be counterintuitive, especially in a time when federal revenues are stretched because of military obligations and unanticipated natural disasters. At the same time, it's obvious that lowering taxes stimulates business growth, because there's more money to go around. And business growth yields means that there's more taxable activity going on, so government revenues also grow. If government spending is restrained at the same time, you have a win-win situation.

It should be a commonsense economic strategy to stop taxing people to death. With your common sense, you can recognize that if your tax levies are too high, it will be as if you have no tax levy at all, because you will have maxed out the revenue benefits. Businesses will struggle and shrivel because the economy is in trouble, and there's not as much left to tax.

You can generate the same amount of revenue by levying high taxes on low production or by imposing lower taxes on high production. National leaders who have the national interest in mind should always strive for ever-increasing production and the consequent creation of wealth. The ideal ratio of taxes to income may be difficult to agree upon, but the goal should be one that has the potential for yielding the best results for both the taxpayers and the government.

Here is the basic footprint of my approach to tax policy, which I will flesh out in the rest of the chapter:

- Our tax code should be *pro-growth*. It should reward entrepreneurs, and it should give people incentives to save and invest.

- *Corporate taxes should be lowered,* to enable American businesses to better compete in the global economy.

- Our *tax code should be greatly simplified and shortened.* I believe we should take radical steps to adopt a flatter, fairer tax policy.

I will discuss each of these points briefly, coalescing my thoughts in the final section about a tax policy that is known as "flat tax," which seems to me to be the best way to achieve these goals.

Pro-Growth Thinking

Economic growth is achieved by increasing economic resources. More resources translate into more output and higher productivity. And an improved economic climate goes hand-in-hand with job creation (which means that economic growth is pumped up some more).

With increased resources, business opportunities increase. Entrepreneurs can capture a foothold and get a leg up. The word *entrepreneur* means "to undertake." It is related to the word *enterprise.* Entrepreneurs are people with initiative, enterprising people who are willing to undertake business risk for the sake of achieving a goal. To quote Jack Kemp, "Enterprising men and women are the source of all wealth, jobs, technology, and new ideas."[1]

With more business activity, we get higher economic growth, and with economic growth, people have the resources to save and invest. They no longer need every penny they earn for their basic expenditures. It's possible for them to build up reserves, and those reserves, when invested, result in more growth for the economy. Saving and investment are desirable from a personal, corporate, or governmental point of view.

We need more jobs, especially in my state of Michigan. The GOP has become identified as the party of economic growth, and I want to do everything in my power to maintain the upward momentum, making it not only possible for companies and citizens to engage in meaningful employment, but also allowing that increased employment to propel the economy to new levels of robustness.

The bottom line is that lowering taxes promotes economic growth, and one clearly positive ramification of lower taxes is an increase of resources on the individual and the business level.

Improve the Climate for Global Competition

American businesses are taxed at the highest corporate tax rate in the world, an incredible 35 percent. Those taxes must be lowered.

At this high rate, companies cannot compete in a global economic environment. Such high taxation causes American businesses to pull up stakes and establish headquarters overseas. Not only do such high taxes encourage the outsourcing of jobs and interfere with the competitive pricing of goods, but they also encourage the "outsourcing" or exportation of another valuable commodity, namely *cash.*

In America, we have grown used to hearing the voices of labor unions, who want to protect existing jobs. They and the liberal intellectuals dominate discussions, favoring ever-expanding regulation over the natural give-and-take of free market competition. Meantime, litigation has run amok, further deterring investment in the creation of jobs at home.

Speaking as a potential legislator from Michigan, the birthplace of the auto industry, I will fight for keeping jobs in my state, but I will also contend for an improved business environment, which represents the best tactic for stemming the job losses and creating new jobs. Whether that means cutting taxes or giving tax credits to companies who hire, retain, or retrain American workers in my state or other states, I am for it.

Let's lower capital gains taxes, which manacle American businesses and discourage investing. Alan Greenspan, former chairman of the Federal Reserve, has testified that the best tax rate for capital gains would be zero, because much greater entrepreneurial incentive is provided by tax-free capital gains.[2] By taxing capital gains, we tax investment. By taxing investment, we hobble progress. As I noted above, entrepreneurial activity translates into more jobs, a stronger economy, and greater overall wealth. This is commonsense thinking.

Our current tax policies create an environment in which American companies become the attractive targets of takeovers by companies from overseas. (Think Daimler-Chrysler. It's not Chrysler-Daimler because it would have been disadvantageous for the American company to acquire the German one.) Let's make a point of creating a tax policy that draws businesses from around the globe. The competition is unfavorable as long as corporations based in the United States are hobbled tax-wise.

While we're at it, let's dispense with the death tax. It's morally reprehensible, opportunistic. You pay taxes faithfully all your life and you manage to amass a little nest egg. Then when you die, the government can tax away up to 60 percent of it, leaving your children almost empty-handed.

Killer Tax Code

Have you ever taken a look at the United States tax code? It's on the large side.

The greatest political documents in the world are the Declaration of Independence and the Constitution. Together, they are about 6,000 words long. (The Constitution consists of 4,543 words, including the signatures, and the Declaration of Independence has 1,458 words.)

The greatest book that was ever written is the Holy Bible. It contains about 750,000 words.

And the greatest job-killing and economy-killing document in the world is the United States tax code—which weighs in at over 9,000,000 words (more than 60,000 pages)—and is growing daily!

Nobody can read it. In fact, if you could read it at a rate of 400 words per minute (which would be pretty good, considering the density of the material), it would take you more than 47 eight-hour working days to plow through it. That's a month and a half! Is it any wonder that tax-preparers and even the IRS itself tend to make mistakes all the time?

Here's a sample of what the tax code is like:

TITLE 26 ▪ Subtitle A ▪ CHAPTER 1 ▪ Subchapter A ▪ PART III ▪ § 15

§ 15. Effect of changes. Release date: 2005-08-31

(a) General rule

If any rate of tax imposed by this chapter changes,

and if the taxable year includes the effective date of the change (unless that date is the first day of the taxable year), then—

(1) tentative taxes shall be computed by applying the rate for the period before the effective date of the change, and the rate for the period on and after such date, to the taxable income for the entire taxable year; and

(2) the tax for such taxable year shall be the sum of that proportion of each tentative tax which the number of days in each period bears to the number of days in the entire taxable year.

(b) Repeal of tax

For purposes of subsection (a)—

(1) if a tax is repealed, the repeal shall be considered a change of rate; and

(2) the rate for the period after the repeal shall be zero.

(c) Effective date of change

For purposes of subsections (a) and (b)—

(1) if the rate changes for taxable years "beginning after" or "ending after" a certain date, the following day shall be considered the effective date of the change; and

(2) if a rate changes for taxable years "beginning on or after" a certain date, that date shall be considered the effective date of the change.

(d) Section not to apply to inflation adjustments

This section shall not apply to any change in rates under subsection (f) of section 1 (relating to adjustments in tax tables so that inflation will not result in tax increases).

(e) References to highest rate

If the change referred to in subsection (a) involves a change in the highest rate of tax imposed by section 1 or 11 (b), any reference in this chapter to such highest rate (other than in a provision imposing a tax by reference to such rate) shall be treated as a reference to the weighted average of the highest rates before and after the change determined on the basis of the respective portions of the taxable year before the date of the change and on or after the date of the change.

(f) Rate reductions enacted by Economic Growth and Tax Relief Reconciliation Act of 2001

This section shall not apply to any change in rates under subsection (i) of section 1 (relating to rate reductions after 2000).[3]

Had enough? I think I've made my point.

The tax system we are using has become a multi-headed monster. It needs to be completely scrapped. If I had my way, I would make all tax-filing as simple as the government's online e-filing system. You should be able to fill out a form that would fit on a postcard.

The United States tax code should have one rate for everyone who is above the poverty line. We should all be able to pay roughly the same rate. The law should allow exemptions only for the following:

1. For *children* (because children are a valuable resource)

2. For *elderly dependents* (because caretakers should be compensated)

3. For *college students* (to incentivize higher education)

4. For *military service* (because of the personal sacrifice)

5. For *home mortgages* (to encourage home ownership)

6. For *charitable giving* (because nonprofit organizations are doing essential work deserving of support)

Our tax policy should reflect the fact that the family is the foundational unit of our society. We would do well to increase the per-child tax exemption to give families relief from some of the high cost of raising a family. The children of our nation are our greatest national resource.

We have a killer tax system. When you combine inflation with our current system of progressive tax rates, you kill risk, you kill saving, you kill investment, and you kill business initiative. People are propelled into unwelcome higher tax brackets with little to show for it in terms of their real income. So what if you have fewer deductions? The net benefit can be eaten away by inflation. Ordinary citizens can still find themselves in tax brackets that used to be proprietary to the landed gentry.

There is a way out of this mess, although it will make Washington's "K Street" (the lawyer-lobbyist crowd) unhappy, and countless seasonal tax-preparers may have to look for another line of work. It's called the flat tax, and it has become the rallying cry for a growing number of bipartisan supporters. The flat tax solution is *achievable*.

Flat Tax Reform

What is a flat tax, and how would it improve the situation? How would a flatter, fairer, and simpler tax look?

The idea of replacing the impossibly complex and burdensome federal income tax system with a flat tax is not a new one, but it is coming to people's attention because of a large number and range of current tax reform proposals that are on the table, many of which include some form of a flat tax. A viable flat tax reform proposal should include the following features.

The flat tax is a single-rate federal tax on personal income and corporate profits. Did you get that? A single-rate tax. No more tax brackets. Everyone is in the same bracket. The flat tax would simplify everything. It would be indisputably fair.

Personal income and corporate profits would be taxed "close to the source," and money would not be taxed again.

In other words, your earned interest and dividends would not be taxed—the tax on those profits would have been paid at the corporate level, and the corporations would no longer have a deduction for interest payments. If you are a retired person, your Social Security payments and any after-tax-funded retirement vehicles would be tax-free. You would have paid taxes on that money the first time, when you earned it.

No more alternative minimum tax (AMT). The flat rate would apply across the board to everyone.

The current corporate tax rate of 35 percent would be cut down. Companies would pay the same percentage on their profits as individuals pay on their personal income. (Profits are the total revenue of the company minus salaries/wages, purchases of materials, plant improvements, and equipment.) Corporations could dispense with depreciation schedules and credits. Their purchases could be written off right when the purchase was made. Whatever a company would spend for its physical plant and equipment would offset taxable income for the same year in which the purchase was made. A 100 percent write-off provision favors business activity.

The death tax would be repealed for good. No longer would your life savings, upon which taxes have already been paid, be subjected to a second (usually large) tax helping. (As they say, "No taxation without respiration.")

The flat tax includes a basic set of six exemptions and credits as I have listed above, with more generous provisions and limits than we have at present. Enough of your income should remain tax-free so that you can maintain an adequate standard of living. We need to make sure that low-income workers pay less—sometimes zero—in taxes. According to the Forbes' flat tax model, by the year 2010, 65 million returns, which is 42 percent of all returns, would not owe any tax at all.[4]

The current tax credit refund feature would remain. In other words, when a family's child tax credit is more than the amount of taxes they owe, they would get the credit amount in the form of a refund, even when they have not paid any taxes.

The Earned Income Tax Credit (EITC) would also remain, for the benefit of families with lower incomes, to encourage them to stay in the workforce instead of applying for public assistance.

The flat tax would not change Medicare and Social Security taxes. Of course, since the flat tax would be a federal tax, it would not change your local taxes or state taxes. However, it would eliminate the more than 9,000,000-word federal tax code that shows no signs of improvement otherwise.

Benefits of the Flat Tax

First, you really would be able to fill out your forms for a flat tax in a few minutes, and the form you would fill out really would fit on a single sheet of paper, or even a postcard.

With the flat tax, lower-income taxpayers would be safe from taxes. All citizens would have more financial autonomy and less government oversight. This is much fairer than the current system of progressive tax rates.

Theory would translate into practice with the adoption of the flat tax—without taxation on investment and savings, investment would increase. That means improvement for individual lifestyles as well as for the national economy. And without a tax on dividends, companies would raise their dividends even more than they have as a result of the dividend tax reduction of May 2003.

Another advantage: companies that currently face great overseas competitive disadvantages would no longer pay taxes in whatever country they do business as well as in the United States. Under the flat tax, their American taxes would be paid only on profits earned within the borders of the United States. This levels the playing field for American companies, since currently they must compete with foreign companies who enjoy this single-tax benefit.

Interest rates would decrease under a flat-tax system. Without an interest tax, lenders don't require such high payments.

With the flat tax, the government would receive increased revenues. In the past, when the progressive rates have been pared down, economic prosperity has resulted (more about that below).

Then there's the immense benefit in terms of tax compliance. How much time (and you know that time = money) have you squandered on tax-filing? How long is the wait for an appointment with your local tax-preparer? How much effort and expense do wealthier individuals and corporations put into tax avoidance, locating and squeezing through loopholes in the tax code? How much must be paid in legal fees in the effort to sort out disputes?

Today, a ridiculous amount of the gross domestic product (GDP) is spent on tax compliance. The nonpartisan Congressional Budget Office puts it at 18 percent of the GDP. Tax compliance includes everything from money paid to accountants and administrative staffs to time-consuming political "discussions" about our oppressively complex tax policy. According to studies, the average small business shells out $724 to collect and remit $100 in taxes.[5] Such a waste of time and money is unconscionable. The flat tax would eliminate enough red tape to backfill the Gulf of Mexico. The vastly reduced costs of tax compliance would translate into benefits for individuals as well as for corporations.

The end result would be good for everyone, including the federal government. The economic status of individuals and corporations would improve, which translates into greater incentives, investment, job creation, and the subsequent creation of more wealth. All of the increase would be taxed at the same flat rate, which would further encourage growth. It would take only a few years to see much higher government revenues.

Flat Tax Track Record

Other countries operate successfully with a flat tax system; therefore, a track record has been established. Hong Kong, for example, has had a flat tax since 1947. Because this approach to tax-levying solves so many problems, flat tax systems are currently under consideration not only in the United States but also in Germany, China, Spain, Croatia, and elsewhere.

Naturally, revamping the tax system is not the only consideration in an evaluation of economic benefits, but the track record established by other flat-tax countries shows an impressive pattern of growth. Flat taxes are simple, and the rates are generally lower than those imposed by progressive tax systems. Countries that employ the flat tax system boost their economies and encourage outside business investment. The flat tax system improves the competitive edge of any country that adopts it.

Past tax cuts in the United States provide us with insight into the potential benefits of the tax cuts that are part of a flat tax system. Fiscal policy always has a strong positive impact on the health of a national economy. Taking a quick survey, we find out that:[6]

- When Calvin Coolidge slashed the top tax rate from 73 percent to 25 percent between 1921 and 1926, national economic growth improved by over 6 percent and personal income tax revenues rose by more than 61 percent.

- When John F. Kennedy brought the top tax rate down from 91 percent to 70 percent between 1963 and 1965, the economy expanded by 42 percent (more than 5 percent per year by 1968), and federal tax revenue increased by 62 percent.

- When Ronald Reagan cut the top tax rate from 70 percent to 28 percent between 1980 and 1988, the nation enjoyed a 4 percent economic growth rate, and tax revenue grew 99.4 percent.

When tax rates are lowered, what seems to happen is that high-bracket taxpayers, logically, take money out of tax-sheltered investments and from consumption and turn it into more highly productive (and taxable) investments. Also, quite simply, people become less tax-evasive; there is less reason to try to avoid taxes.[7] The flat tax is good for taxpayers, and it is good for the tax collectors as well.

Radical and Promising

The flat tax system would represent long-overdue radical surgery on the federal government. It would not be fatal to the patient—far from it. Tax simplification would improve fairness and economic efficiency.

If we can achieve tax simplification, we can better address other nagging problems such as urban development. We can put urban business development within the reach of motivated individuals who currently cannot afford to invest in the inner city. The elimination of capital gains enhances equity investment and business development in areas of high unemployment. Business development means job creation. I wonder what our deteriorating inner cities would look like if businesses began to return and the tax base began to grow again?

I'm on the bandwagon for tax reform. I support President Bush's plan to make tax cuts permanent. But I want to take it a lot further. The time is ripe and bipartisan agreement is coming together for a pioneering and sweeping change in the tax policies of the United States of America. Let's make it happen.

CHAPTER 5

WINNING THE IMMIGRATION WARS

ALL OF US—BY WAY OF OUR ANCESTORS IF NOT DIRECTLY WITHIN OUR OWN LIFETIMES—CAME TO AMERICA FROM SOMEWHERE ELSE. MY PEOPLE CAME FROM AFRICA BY SLAVE SHIPS. OTHERS CAME FROM EUROPE OR ASIA, FROM NORTH OR SOUTH AMERICA. EVEN THE NATIVE AMERICANS CAME, THOUSANDS OF YEARS AGO, FROM SOMEWHERE ELSE. THE GENIUS OF AMERICA IS ITS MELTING-POT ABILITY TO ASSIMILATE PEOPLE FROM A MULTITUDE OF CULTURES.

Contemporary immigration patterns are changing America's racial and ethnic complexion. Thirty years ago, most Americans could be labeled "black" or "white," but that is no longer the case. Even without increased immigration from Asia, Central and South America, and the Middle East, the increasing level of intermarriage between groups has resulted in a blended, multiracial population.

Children who are born in the United States, with a few exceptions, become American citizens by virtue of their place of birth. It doesn't matter if their parents are citizens or not. The Fourteenth Amendment to the Constitution guarantees this right, stating that "all persons born or naturalized in the United States, and subject to the jurisdiction thereof, are citizens of the United States."

Adults who want to become U.S. citizens must first obtain legal permanent resident status. The whole process of immigration to naturalization can be long and difficult. The U.S. Citizenship and Immigration Services has had a serious backlog and has been criticized for its slowness in responding to applications from immigrants for work authorizations, permanent residencies, and naturalization. However, in 2004 alone, improved procedures within the agency reduced the backlog by 2.3 million cases.[1] Because the United States Congress has been vested with the authority to enact and modify laws concerning the naturalization process, I intend to keep an eye on this situation to make sure it continues to work better and to see how the system can be streamlined further.

We Need Immigrants

The present-day influx of immigrants—both legal and illegal—has not been this high since the 1920s.[2] We should welcome immigrants. I believe that America needs more good citizens. If for no other reason, we need them to replace the citizens we have lost to abortion. It's common sense to me that if we abort a million-plus people every year and thus deprive ourselves of that national resource, we need to increase legal immigration to make up for it.

What we have seen in the technological, scientific, and medical communities is that without the immigration of highly qualified candidates, especially from South Asia, India, and Pakistan, our academic institutions, hospitals, engineering facilities, and scientific research labs would not have enough staff. Yes, we should be improving our own public education in order to produce more qualified graduates, but this is one place where the melting pot is working well.

One controversial aspect of the immigration/naturalization process is the assimilation of people from other cultures into the American culture. Should we become a bi- or trilingual nation? Should we celebrate everybody's national holidays? How much should we emphasize American history and the way the democratic process functions? How "diverse" should we be? How diverse can we afford to be?

English spoken here

I feel strongly that if you come to this country legally, *you* are the person who should change, not the country where you have come to live. So I believe in English-only courses. American life and American business are based on the English language, and today's immigrants, just as the immigrants that came before them, can only be assimilated into the society by learning English and then by passing a course in American history before being sworn in as citizens. English language proficiency and an understanding of the workings of American government and economy are essential to upward mobility in the United States of America.

In addition, assimilated immigrants need to understand basic American values. For example, we have religious tolerance in this country. We are not a police state. But we do have laws that control, for example, the way we treat women and children. Husbands can only have one wife at a time in America, and you may not beat your wife or your children. You can send your children to public school through the twelfth grade here without paying tuition, but a university education is costly. You must drive on the right side of the road, and you must stop at red lights.

The Hispanic Population

In the U.S. census of 2003, Hispanics were found to outnumber blacks for the first time. Their population numbers are projected to rise both because of immigration (both legal and illegal) and high birth rates.

I don't have any problem whatsoever with *legal* immigration from Mexico and other Spanish-speaking countries. I don't even have a problem with the idea that Mexicans in particular want to find work in the United States without becoming citizens.

What I do have a problem with is the flood of *illegal* immigration that we are seeing. This is the first time in the history of America that we have had such an enormous concentration of illegal immigrants. Because they are so concentrated, they can essentially create a "little Mexico" wherever they live. Many of them, even as they enter the second generation, are not becoming assimilated into American culture at all. They have no incentive to do so. Practically speaking, their illegal status, within enclaves of people who are in the same situation, is a deterrent to assimilation.

They are something like a permanent-transitory group—as much as 11 million strong (nobody knows for sure). According to the Pew Hispanic Center, illegal immigration increased by 23 percent from 2001 to 2005, and 57 percent of the undocumented aliens were from Mexico.[3] This is in spite of better-funded border patrolling that has been in place since the 2001 terrorist attacks in New York and Washington.

An analysis of census data by the Migration Policy Institute shows that Mexican-born immigrants have an unemployment rate that outstrips the overall unemployment rate of foreign-born immigrants from other countries combined with the unemployment rate for U.S.-born internationals *and* for the total population of the United States.[4] That is a huge disparity, and it represents a serious problem.

As a result of these facts, it is impossible to dispute the fact that the illegal immigration problem is largely a Hispanic one. I see this illegal immigration as a threat both to the economic security of American society as well as to our homeland security.

The Economic Price of Illegal Immigration

The brunt of the economic price for illegal immigration is being carried by the western and some of the southern states, especially in the form of health care and general social benefits. Minorities comprise more than 50 percent of the population under the age of eighteen in Arizona, California, Hawaii, New Mexico, and Texas, as well as in certain large cities such as Los Angeles, Miami, and Houston.[5] Their public educational systems are overwhelmed by children whose parents came here illegally.

Health-care costs

Hospitals in the United States, concentrated especially heavily in these geographical regions, provide about $34 billion worth of uncompensated care a year.[6] According to Paul Fronstin, director of the Employee Benefit Research Institute's Health Research and

Education Program, "Immigrants accounted for about one-third of the increase in the uninsured between 1994 and 1998, but between 1998 and 2003 they accounted for 86 percent of the increase. To the degree that immigration continues to increase, it is likely that the uninsured will also continue to increase."[7] Here are two more alarming statistics cited in an article in the *Miami Herald*:[8]

- In Los Angeles County, where the department of health is running a deficit of $1.2 billion, nearly two million illegal immigrants crowd its emergency rooms, creating long waits for patients, forcing the closure of many facilities.

- The U.S.-Mexico Border Counties Coalition reported that in just twenty-four counties on the southern border [of the United States], the cost of uncompensated care for illegal aliens totals more than $200 million every year.

Legislators in one state (Alabama) decided that their best recourse for redressing this imbalance would be to ask for compensation from the federal government for the unpaid health-care costs. Their logic is simple: the federal government is supposed to secure the border. Since the border is not secure, their health-care system (as with other border states) is sinking under the load of uncompensated health care, mostly provided in the form of expensive emergency room visits. They feel it is time for the federal government to help fix the situation. Perhaps this is a good way for other states to send a strong message to the United States Congress to address the problem of illegal immigration.

The states that are most affected by the impact of illegal immigration on health-care costs include California, Arizona, New Mexico, Texas, Florida, and North Carolina. A handful of northern states are also suffering from this imbalance.

Poverty rates

Because so many immigrants (both legal and illegal) come into the United States poor and unskilled, poverty rates in America have remained higher than they would be otherwise. A quarter of the people who live below the poverty line are Hispanics, and since 1989, Hispanics have made up almost three quarters of the increase in people who live in poverty.

The poverty represented by immigration has also been keeping the nation's median income flat for five years and counting, which represents the longest stretch of a non-rising median, ever.[9]

Depressed wages

You've heard it said that we need illegal immigrants because there are certain low-level jobs that Americans just will not do. I don't believe that's strictly true. However, there are jobs that Americans will not do for illegal immigrant *wages.* The presence of so many illegal immigrants depresses the wages to the point that the market cannot operate as it should. If we did something about the illegal workers, the wages would have to rise. Guess what would happen next? Eventually, those same jobs would start to look attractive to unemployed Americans, who would say, "I know this is hard work, but I'm going to get paid enough for it, so I'll do it."

Full Border Security

Because of the multifaceted negative impact of illegal immigration, we cannot afford to delay the remedial measures that are so urgently needed. We *must* have full border security. I believe we must close our borders completely to illegal entry by whatever means necessary, including the use of military force.

Full border security does not preclude the use of a system of paying fines, whereby illegal immigrants can make restitution and start off again on the right foot. But I don't think it should be easy to get off the hook. Just because Mexico is our close neighbor, we shouldn't privilege Mexican illegal immigrants over legal immigrants from other countries. Neither should we throw up our hands and give up the fight just because there are so many of them. Illegal immigration needs to be controlled, and stopped, and I believe it's possible.

Border security has been improved greatly already, although obviously more needs to be done. Walls and fences have been erected; border patrol officers have been hired and provided with better equipment. Trade with Mexico has increased, and the overall welfare within that country has improved. Perhaps in the distant future, we will reach the point where it no longer makes as much sense to come to the United States for economic reasons.

But a lot more needs to be done. The Immigration and Naturalization Service should "card" employers, checking the identification documents of their workers—and readily deport illegal immigrants. Currently, employer sanctions are lax. To make a tougher system work successfully, we need to institute stiff fines for employers who hire illegal immigrants.

We also need to improve the security of the identification documents. Right now, it's far too easy to forge them. We should model new identification documents on the I.D. systems that are being used successfully in airports throughout the nation. Since January 2004, more than 25 million visitors with visas have come through United States Immigration and Customs Enforcement portals, and almost 600 criminals or immigration violators have been fingered—literally, since the system relies on biometric data collected from finger scans. Since the US-VISIT (United States Visitor and Immigrant Status Indicator Technology) program was instituted, more than 7,000 visas were denied before applicants ever came to our shores.[10]

If we had completely sealed borders, not only with Mexico but also with Canada, it would be necessary to arrest illegal aliens and deport them within days, without recourse to the U.S. court system. It should be the law: if you don't have the right documents, you leave on the next bus.

Immigration Quotas

We need to establish immigration quotas for Mexicans. Among other things, this would send a clear message to Mexico that the substantial flow of remittances from the illegal workers in the United States back to Mexico could no longer be depended upon as it has been for the past thirty years. But if we established quotas for legal immigrants, we'd also have to change current immigration law regarding family unification provisions, because it is the primary basis upon which Hispanic immigrants enter the country legally at this time. We wouldn't want non-family applicants to be unfairly squeezed out between quotas and the family provisions.

The illegal immigrant situation is out of control. We've tried the amnesty approach, and it didn't work. Of course, each time federal amnesty is extended, the contingencies have never been enacted, so we have cleared the decks with a blanket amnesty, but we have not carried through with the necessary improvements to the system.

The liberals have it wrong when they say that the Fourteenth Amendment guarantees the same rights to illegal aliens as to legal citizens of the United States. I don't think so.

Domestic Security Threats

Another threat from illegal immigration is the danger to our domestic security. In spite of much-increased security efforts since 9/11, it can be relatively easy for a terrorist or a terrorist sympathizer to enter this country. *Porous* is the operative word for our borders, not only our border with Mexico but also our border with Canada and our coastal ports of entry.

Even with increased funding, equipping and hiring of agents, better strategies for border security, and tighter airport and seaport security, the United States government has failed to prevent 800,000 people per year from entering the country illegally.[11]

Porter Goss, director of the Central Intelligence Agency (CIA), testified in April 2005 about the serious potential for hostile infiltration via our unsecured borders. Here is part of his testimony before the House Subcommittee on International Terrorism and Nonproliferation:

> Once [nuclear components have been] secured, terrorists may try to smuggle a nuclear weapon into the United States using the routes by which large quantities of contraband are routinely smuggled into our country. I am particularly concerned about our porous borders, where we need to improve security quickly.[12]

If the problem is so obvious to everyone, why does Congress drag its feet when it comes to doing something about it? The answer is, as you might expect, "politics." Apparently it is not politically correct to brand a problem with the name of a people-group. If you start to talk about this problem of the porous U.S. border and its potential for enemy infiltration, then you're talking about specific nationalities. Before you know what's happening, the liberals label you a bigot of some sort. "You're anti-Hispanic." "You use racial profiling." "You don't want to give poor folks a chance in the land of opportunity."

It's difficult to occupy an elected office when your ratings take a beating in the polls because you have adopted an unpopular cause. And yet—why not? Our national security is definitely at stake.

Keeping Out Criminals

The terrorist threat dominates the discussion, but let us remember that our domestic security is also threatened by garden variety criminals. The world is populated with a large number of people with good intentions—and a considerable number of people with bad ones. They don't have to be carrying a nuclear device or a dirty bomb to want to try to penetrate our defenses. Some are pedophiles, murderers, drug addicts, thieves, individuals without consciences.

Fewer foreign visitors with criminal records will make it through our new "US-VISIT" security clearance program. A press release from the U.S. Immigration and Customs Enforcement Agency (ICE) includes the following notes:[13]

- On May 8, 2005, ICE agents at the Lewiston, NY port of entry arrested David Kricheli, a native of the Republic of Georgia who was wanted for murder in Germany....Kricheli had been living in Canada for years under a new identity and had obtained a job as a truck driver, routinely crossing into the United States.

- On May 15, 2005, CBP [U.S. Customs and Border Protection] inspectors at Los Angeles International Airport encountered a Swiss national seeking admission....A US-VISIT fingerprint check by CBP inspectors revealed that this person was wanted by Interpol as he is suspected of pedophilia.

- A routine US-VISIT check of a visitor's fingerprints by a CBP inspector at John F. Kennedy International Airport revealed that the visitor was using an alias. Further CBP checks showed that he had two prior arrests for drug trafficking, a subsequent failure to appear in court, and visa fraud. The traveler presented a fraudulent visa he had used to enter the United States more than sixty times without being detected by standard biographic record checks.

- A cooperative effort between the ICE agents in New York and CBP inspectors in St. Thomas, Virgin Islands, led to the apprehension of a St. Lucia native who was the subject of a US-VISIT biometric "lookout," with a warrant for his arrest for the rape of a fourteen-year-old girl. The subject attempted to enter the United States as a visitor for pleasure through the St. Thomas port of entry and was immediately taken into custody by CBP inspectors. He was later extradited to New York to face prosecution.

As I mentioned above, if such a program were adopted by our border protection agencies in conjunction with a policy of tighter security all around, many more criminals could be denied entry to the United States before they can disappear into the back alleys of one of our big cities.

The issue of border control and national security is complex and huge. No longer can we afford to have borders that permit illegal aliens to enter as they wish to do.

No one disputes that we have a problem. We only need leaders who have the courage to do something about it.

CHAPTER 6

HELPING FELLOW AMERICANS

THE NUMBER OF AMERICANS WHO NOW LIVE BELOW THE POVERTY LINE (WHICH, FOR A FAMILY OF FOUR, MEANS HAVING AN INCOME OF LESS THAN $19,300) IS ABOUT 12.7 PERCENT. WHEN MEDICARE WAS ESTABLISHED IN 1965, THE POVERTY RATE WAS ABOUT 19 PERCENT. DURING THOSE FORTY YEARS, THE POVERTY RATE AMONG AFRICAN AMERICANS HAS DECLINED MUCH MORE SHARPLY THAN IT HAS AMONG OTHER DEMOGRAPHIC GROUPS—FROM 55 PERCENT IN 1959 TO LESS THAN 25 PERCENT IN 2004. ALTHOUGH these rates are still too high, many factors have played into this improvement.

Government programs have expanded to include Medicaid, food stamps, housing subsidies, the Earned Income Tax Credit (EIT), and Supplemental Security Income. The charge that social programs tend to trap the poor in dependency and deny them the power to control their lives has led to the redesign of certain federal programs. For example, the government has been allowing tenants of public housing projects to buy the buildings and take over their management.

In 1996, the United States Congress overhauled the welfare system. The Welfare Reform Act, by establishing more stringent work requirements, cut the number of families receiving traditional welfare from 5 million in 1994 to 2 million in 2003.[1] Aid to Families with Dependent Children was replaced with state-run assistance programs financed by federal grants. The new law also limits lifetime welfare assistance to five years. Most able-bodied adults are required to work after two years on welfare. Food stamps are limited to a period of three months unless the recipients are working, and welfare benefits have been eliminated for legal immigrants who have not become U.S. citizens.[2]

Obviously, even the best government-based social programs are limited in what they can provide. One of their great failings is the inevitable paternalistic tendency to maintain people in mere survival mode instead of helping them to improve their lot in life.

Government programs provide few incentives and no rewards for individuals who may be able to become self-sufficient. Americans who are poor, abused, disabled, or addicted can receive valuable government aid, but there is a cost to it. That cost is hope.

Without the missing ingredient of hope, the cycle of poverty cannot be broken.

The public assistance provided by the federal government needs to incorporate some way of restoring hope and enabling people to rise above survival mode. This needs to occur both within existing programs as well as in the context of new endeavors, such as government collaborations with faith-based assistance programs. In fact, it is from the latter that the hope component is rising up the most strongly in this first decade of the twenty-first century.

Improving Government Programs

Government assistance programs tend to become top-heavy. Like an overgrown apple orchard, the quantity and quality of the valuable fruit is seriously compromised unless this perennial problem is addressed on a regular basis. However, even with regular pruning, the built-in bureaucracy supersedes the compassionate touch in government social assistance programs, and it may not be possible to address this lack to a very high degree. Nevertheless, each program could be improved, and new programs can be instituted to fill needs that are not being addressed.

A range of potential improvements could include the following:

1. To better provide for children trapped in violent homes, especially homes characterized by drugs or crime, the government could provide options that are as radical as the home circumstances are dire—for instance, sending the children to faith-based boarding schools such as the well-known Girls and Boys Town in Nebraska and other states.

2. To enhance the education process, the government could encourage programs that provide monetary incentives for poor inner-city kids.

3. To help conquer violence and promote public safety, the government could support neighborhood watch groups.

4. To improve their future chances, first-time offenders, could be provided with rehabilitation from addictions or other problems, as well as with vocational training. (This is happening to some degree via government collaboration with nonprofit organizations in the private sector.)

5. To better follow up on violent ex-prisoners, they should be required by the terms of

their parole to wear electronic surveillance bracelets. Faith-based programs could be recruited to play a major rule in the parole process for every prisoner, especially young first offenders.

6. To stem the erosion of decency in American culture, the federal government should crack down on obscenity, indecency, and violence on the public airwaves as well as in interstate commerce. The Federal Communications Commission has made a start, but much more needs to be undertaken.

Besides improving existing social assistance programs, the federal minimum wage, which has not been increased for eight years now, should be a high priority for Congress. Although some states have established higher minimum wage amounts, the current federal minimum of $5.15 per hour level is insufficient. In fact, when measured against the average living wage for nonsupervisory positions, the current level represents a fifty-six-year low.[3] A higher federal minimum wage would help more families and individuals rise above the poverty level. Unskilled workers who earn the minimum wage continue to qualify for government programs such as food stamps. Even those who do not want to depend on government assistance cannot earn a living wage.

Government Health-Care Initiatives

Have you asked anyone lately for his or her opinion of the American health-care system? Chances are it will be a negative one, especially when you start talking about programs such as Medicare and Medicaid.

These forty-year-old programs are badly in need of streamlining and modification that will make them viable for the next forty years and beyond. Both programs rely on narrowly defined government benefits and diagnostic categories, and they are biased to favor acute care that is reactive and episodic. Medicaid is a joint federal-state program that funds medical care for the poor. The requirements for receiving Medicaid and the scope of care available vary widely from state to state. At a cost of about $156 billion a year, Medicaid is the nation's largest social-welfare program. Medicare, another form of federal health insurance, pays a large part of the medical bills incurred by Americans who are sixty-five and older or who are disabled, regardless of age. Medicare is financed by a portion of the Social Security tax, by premiums paid by recipients, and by federal funds. Everyone who receives Social Security payments is covered by Medicare.

Medicare is a bureaucratic dinosaur. Recipients of benefits don't realize that Medicare cannot possibly keep up with rapidly developing research and that, as a consequence, they are being shortchanged by being locked into a certain set of covered procedures.

In addition, both Medicare and Medicaid operate with outdated third-party payment procedures, and both have grown larger than original fiscal projections. The federal government needs to cut out the bureaucratic fat as quickly as possible to keep Medicare afloat, and the states need to do the same for Medicaid.

Nothing will improve with government-provided health aid unless we wrestle with several aspects of the systems. One aspect has to do with information systems. America is past due with regards to updating medical records, creating and storing as much as possible electronically. Witness the chaos after Hurricane Katrina to see how, among other factors, irretrievable and scattered paper records can hobble an entire health-care network. Filing cabinets in hospital basements are not a good solution. One disaster is enough to show us that we need to change something, and the federal government may be in the best position to mandate the change to a more nimble and accessible system of integrated electronic records. Time will tell whether or not the government will take up the challenge before the next disaster strikes.

Another commonsense improvement that could have major long-term benefits is the simple addition of preventive features to government medical assistance programs. If you are a beneficiary and you demonstrate that you are living a healthy lifestyle, you should be able to accrue extra funding with which to purchase health benefits that are not covered by the government plan (thus enhancing your health further). To achieve healthier lifestyles and to cut the outlay of payments for medical services, beneficiaries should be introduced to programs for weight loss, exercise, and smoking cessation. Such programs are cost effective.

With the likelihood that more and more Americans will have longer lives, attention should be shifted to supporting smart choices. Senior Americans who participate in life-enhancing programs enjoy better physical and emotional health.

Older Americans are increasing their use of the Internet and will continue to do so. Therefore, the information about Medicare and Medicaid that is available online, such as comparisons of hospitals, doctors, and treatment options, should continue to be improved over time.

Looking at Faith-Based Initiatives

The importance of the link between social assistance sponsored by the government and private (usually faith-based) social assistance cannot be downplayed. The need level is so major and so multifaceted that it requires all the help that can be mustered.

Speaking from a personal point of view as the chief executive of a $30 million operation (Word of Faith includes a church, a private school, and outreach programs such as job training), I see every day how government policies affect people. The thousands of people involved in Word of Faith come from every walk of life.

In the workplace, their job status ranges from unemployed to highly placed executives. Our numerous outreaches keep us in touch with the needs around us. From early on, we determined to contribute to the improvement of the lives of people who otherwise would have only limited help from the state and federal governments. Word of Faith represents a well-developed example of a faith-based institution that offers services to the people in our local area, particularly to those in the African American community.

The term "faith-based initiatives" is somewhat unwieldy, but at least it manages to encompass programs that represent many faiths, not just one or two primary ones. We have become accustomed to the term in the past five years or so because of the social policies of the Bush administration. Obviously, the underlying concept is nothing new; churches and other religious organizations have always provided social services on some scale, because compassionate outreach to fellow human beings is inherent in most belief systems. What is new is the availability of government support for such initiatives.

Faith-Based and Community Initiatives (FBCI) is the name of the White House office that was established in 2001 as a key fulfillment of George W. Bush's campaign promise about "compassionate conservatism." The office coordinates the applications for and disbursal of government funds to nonprofit religious organizations so that they can perform a wide array of services for their clients. The idea itself is simple: faith-based organizations can be more effective in providing social services than can the government, and the government can support them with funding.

To make the federal grants available nationwide, the White House office of FBCI works with separate Centers for Faith-Based and Community Initiatives that have been created within each Cabinet agency—the Departments of Health and Human Services, Housing and Urban Development, Labor, Justice, Agriculture, and Education—and the Agency for International Development. Each center helps applicants with grant descriptions, application instructions, qualifications, and deadlines. The Federal Emergency Management Agency has been directed to allow religious nonprofit disaster-assistance groups to qualify for federal aid after catastrophic events such as hurricanes.

Some states have established bridge positions (faith liaisons) between the local service providers and the government. Consultants in these positions help to bridge the information gap so that government officials and potential collaborators can find out about each other. They also help people outside the government understand the process of grant writing and organize networking conferences.[4]

In fiscal year 2004, competitive grants worth $2 billion were awarded from seven federal agencies to faith-based organizations. A total of 151 programs were benefited, and this number has risen each year, always including many first-time grantees. One goal of the grants is to enable faith-based groups to compete successfully with other social service organizations, ensuring a level playing field at the state and local level, where faith-based and community groups compete with taxpayer-funded social services.

Other goals of the president include asking Congress to enact proposals that provide tax incentives for charitable giving and to extend provisions that protect religious hiring rights, protect the religious rights of beneficiaries, and prevent discrimination against the faith-based entities.[5] In July 2005, President Bush pledged to resume an effort to obtain more corporate donations for faith-based charities.[6]

Faith-based service providers are not allowed to use federal grant or contract money to pay for any "inherently religious" activity, and they must separate "in time or location" any religious activities from government-funded activities. To participate, they do not have to sacrifice the religious character of their organizations, remove religious art or inscriptions from their premises, or change the religious aspects of their organizational title, mission statements, or documents.

Examples of Faith-Based Initiatives

In Rochester, New York, the Frederick Douglass Community Development Corporation, founded by the Memorial AME Church, received more than $5 million from HUD to build a low-income housing project for senior citizens.[7]

A million-dollar grant from the United States Department of Education was used to expand the after-school program in the Columbus, Ohio area, run by St. Stephen's Community House, whose mission statement reflects their commitment to broader social good: "We at St. Stephen's Community House are committed to assisting residents of the Greater Linden area to build community, self-sufficiency, and individual well-being. We assist residents to maximize their potential through programs and services such as employment, social development, community organization, education, and childcare."[8]

In a run-down part of Miami, Florida, the Peacemaker Family Center is a small ministry of Trinity Church that helps unemployed families with low incomes. The center received "seed money" of $50,000 from the Compassion Capital Fund Mini-Grant program, the first federal funding the organization had ever received. The funding proved to be a turning point for the program. They used the money to hire a writer, who helped publicize the worthwhile work of their program, and soon the organization had grown from three employees to twenty-five, thereby expanding their effectiveness proportionately and enabling them to maintain increased funding through increased charitable giving.[9]

These are just a handful of examples of success

through the partnership between the federal government and local faith-based initiatives. You will find faith-based initiatives in every part of the United States, including your own region. Look for them and, if you can, offer your time, donations, and goodwill.

Crime Control

You can't talk about social issues without talking about crime. For the most part, when we hear the word *crime*, we think of illegal activities that physically endanger someone, such as robberies. But there is also white-collar crime. All criminal activities are reprehensible.

I believe that crime comes about for the following reasons:

- There *are* bad people (even though the liberals don't want to believe this). They are found at all levels, from the cutthroat white-collar criminal to the people who pillage, rape, and murder in New Orleans. They are just bad.

- There are people who have been deprived of opportunity who take the course of crime because they believe it's the only way to survive.

- There are greedy people. These people don't *need* to steal anything. It's not a matter of survival. These are highly

> educated people, professionals. They
> know what they're doing, and they know
> it's wrong. I'm talking about corporate,
> white-collar crime.

Regardless of the reasons behind crime, you have to deal with it—severely. That's the only way to do it. Even the "accidental" criminals, the ones who "didn't know any better," need to be dealt with severely. Once they get to the point of committing a crime, it's too late to do anything else. It's a mistake to be soft on crime.

This isn't to say that I don't want to work to improve social and educational circumstances so that fewer people will resort to crime. I believe that crime prevention starts in homes and neighborhood schools. What kind of environment will provide the best possible education for our kids, regardless of where they happen to live? Many times, social problems can be traced to our educational system. If we fixed that, we wouldn't have so much crime or racial unrest.

Crime Control via Faith-Based Initiatives

Crime cuts across race, class, and ethnicity. This is why the efforts of nonprofit organizations are so important. Churches, mosques, and synagogues cut across those same social barriers. In a natural and organic way, faith-based organizations can serve the needs of the people whose lives they touch.

No one knows the people being served better than

the nonprofit organizations that are already doing it. Prison Fellowship (PF) is a great example of one faith-based volunteer initiative that has stepped into the crime arena. Founded by Chuck Colson in 1976, the organization in the United States is the model for others in many countries, making it the most extensive criminal justice ministry in the world. The track record of Prison Fellowship is impressive. PF volunteers offer seminars, counseling, and pen pal programs. Their well-known Angel Tree program pairs the children of inmates with volunteers from churches who provide Christmas gifts for the children that are given on behalf of their incarcerated parents.

The organization provides post-prison support, helping ex-prisoners become reintegrated into community life. An additional program addresses the need for reconciliation between victims and offenders. The PF-sponsored Center for Justice and Reconciliation promotes what they term "restorative justice," and their expert advice has been sought by governments, the United Nations, and other organizations.[10]

Of particular interest in any discussion of crime control and prisons are recidivism statistics—the percentage of former prisoners who recycle back through the prison system because they commit new crimes upon their release. The corrections system in the United States has a high recidivism rate of 67 percent, which, unfortunately, means that our streets are no safer than they were before our prisons got so full. The United

States has the highest incarceration rate in the world, but your chance of becoming the victim of an ex-prisoner is very high.

To counter this trend, Prison Fellowship has partnered with supportive prisons across the nation to create several intensive faith-based programs for inmates. In these programs, a twenty-four-hour prison-within-the-prison is staffed by Prison Fellowship. Astonishingly, since the founding of this InnerChange Freedom Initiative in 1997, the recidivism rate for inmates who have completed the full in-prison and post-prison program is a low 15 percent. This is comparable to a model faith-based program in Brazil called *Humaita,* which has a 16 percent re-arrest rate.[11]

Other successful faith-based initiatives include Operation New Hope and City Center Ministries in Jacksonville, Florida, and the Exodus Transitional Community in East Harlem. Both received funds from the United States Department of Labor for job training for ex-offenders. Upon their release from prison, ex-offenders can sign up for a training course that will prepare them for jobs that exist in the community.[12]

Combining Government Programs With Faith-Based Initiatives

In my opinion, faith-based initiatives represent one of the most effective ways that the federal government has revised public assistance policies. Beyond providing for physical needs, the providers of faith-based initiatives are predisposed to recognize the health- and well-being-providing benefits of spiritual beliefs, not to mention the importance of social ties that can carry a needy person past handouts.

I would like to see present government subsidy programs learn some lessons from faith-based service providers. As I mentioned above, people with disabilities, people who are unemployed, and the elderly need hope and a sense of purpose. One way to provide both is to provide, instead of a series of handouts, some initial assessment of a person's capabilities, followed by help in getting a job. We have entered the information age, and no longer does every injury or a lack of transportation relegate a person to the public dole.

Faith-based programs typically do better than governmental programs at follow-up, likely because the service providers honestly care about their clients. Many of them have a long history of providing tangible services and hope in their local areas. Their programs provide housing, food, clothing, job training, mental health counseling, medical care, parenting education, childcare, and much more. A high percentage of the people who receive comprehensive help from such programs remain self-sufficient afterward.

Faith-Based Initiatives = Common Sense

Volunteerism is on the rise in the United States. It is estimated that almost 50 percent of Americans over age eighteen do volunteer work, and nearly 75 percent of American households contribute money to charity.[13]

I believe that we as Americans have an obligation to help our fellow citizens who are deprived in any way of their God-given rights to life, liberty, and the pursuit of happiness.

President Bush has said:

> Faith-based groups will never replace government when it comes to helping those in need. Yet government must recognize the power and unique contribution of faith-based groups in every part of our country. And when the federal government gives contracts to private groups to provide social services, religious groups should have an equal chance to compete. When decisions are made on public funding, we should not focus on the religion you practice; we should focus on the results you deliver.[14]

Common sense tells us that we should do whatever gives the best results. Faith-based programs do that. They save money. They save heartache for their communities and the nation. They provide foundational stability and decency and reorientation. They strengthen the strong, core, character fiber of the country.

Faith-based organizations should continue to be allowed to partner with the government in specific programs, and their tax exemptions should not be tinkered with. Let's not try to fix what *isn't* broken.

CHAPTER 7

EDUCATION THAT WORKS

Taken as a whole, American education is ranked at or near the bottom of the industrialized world in terms of scores in math, science, engineering, and, strangely enough, even reading. This is an alarming development. At this rate, the United States of America cannot sustain a world-class economy in an information age.

Until fairly recently, our national innovation level has been impressive. Because the efforts of our academic institutions have been combined with well-funded corporate-sponsored research, the United States has produced most of the technological advances that the world now takes for granted: lasers, integrated circuits, computers, the Worldwide Web, fiber optics, wireless communications, global positioning satellites, hospitals full of amazing medical equipment, and so forth. Our rivals in Asia and Europe have taken this as a motivational challenge, and they are gaining on us quickly.

The bipartisan Hart-Rudman Commission (the U.S. Commission on National Security/21st Century) issued the statement in 2001 to the effect that the greatest threat to American security was an attack with a weapon of mass destruction, probably initiated by terrorists. Then they noted that the second-greatest threat to American security was—pay attention to this—the failure of math and science education.

> Americans are living off the economic and security benefits of the last three generations' investment in science and education, but we are now consuming capital. Our systems of basic scientific research and education are in serious crisis, while other countries are redoubling their efforts. In the next quarter century, we will likely see ourselves surpassed, and in relative decline, unless we make a conscious national commitment to maintain our edge.[1]

All of the members of the commission approved a further statement that declared this educational failure to be a greater threat to national security than any conceivable conventional war in the next twenty-five years. If the United States fails to improve and maintain improvement in math and science education, we compromise not only our influence and our standard of living, but also our national security.

This worrisome trend is illustrated by the declining number of American students who have earned PhDs in recent years. In the meantime, other nations, some of which used to be considered third world nations, have greatly expanded the doctoral programs in their own universities. By 2010, China is expected to bypass the United States in terms of the number of science and engineering doctorates awarded by its universities.[2] As recently as 1970, the United States produced more than half of the PhDs in the world. However, projecting from current trends, we will be producing only 15 percent of them within only a few years.[3]

What does this tell us in terms of honing our competitive edge? At this rate, can we survive and thrive economically? The Indian economy is dynamic, and the Chinese economy is growing at a massive rate. These countries and others are our global competitors. We need to become more actively aggressive about the quality and quantity of education that we provide for our citizens. This is not only an issue of education; it is also an issue of economics and an issue of national security.

Mixed Results

We need to rebuild our educational system from the bottom up. As recently as twenty years ago, the United

States ranked first in the world in the percentage of the adult population that held high school and college degrees. Now it ranks ninth among industrialized nations in its share of people with a high school diploma, and seventh in the number who have earned a college degree.[4]

We all pay for faulty education. Besides economic losses to our nation, we pay in terms of social well-being. Undereducated kids are uninspired. They may be intelligent, but if they don't stay in school through the twelfth grade, these bright kids will find it easy to turn to a life of crime. Don't think that the young guy on the street running a vast drug network isn't bright. He's extremely bright. He may be able to add, multiply, and compute better than his counterpart at the university. But he couldn't stick it out in the educational system, so he exploits others instead of becoming a part of the legal economy. His old school system carries a good part of the blame.

As a nation, the price that we pay is exacted down the road if we do not turn out responsible citizens who can think critically, compute, read, and speak at a high level of competence. We wind up taking care of them with public dollars, and we suffer the loss of their entrepreneurial spirit that could have benefited the overall economy. We flush the ingenuity of our young citizens down the drain.

At present, America remains the top-ranking "knowledge economy" in the world, but if the overall education system continues to weaken, this will no longer be the case. When the test scores of American fifteen-year-olds are compared with those of their counterparts in Asia, Europe, and nearby Canada, they fall short. Countries that outperform the United States include Finland, South Korea, the Netherlands, Japan, Canada, and Belgium.[5] Other international surveys show that eighth-graders in the United States are gaining back some of the ground they have lost in science and math. However, fourth-graders' scores have remained flat.[6]

Given what this country as a whole spends on education, these troubling achievement scores reveal that the whole public school system is inefficient and deficient. The average spending per student in the United States is $11,152, which is the second-highest amount in the industrialized world. (Only Switzerland is higher.[7]) Why is all this money not producing equally high results?

International advantage at the college level cannot be maintained if preparatory education in America continues to slip or to remain flat. Barry McGaw, director for education of the thirty-nation Organisation for Economic Co-operation and Development, based in Paris, says, "The very best schools in the U.S. are extraordinary. But the big concern in the U.S. is the diversity of quality of institutions—and the fact that expectations haven't been set high enough."[8] He goes on to say:

The resources devoted to education are among the most important investments that countries and their people make....Both [human and social capital] are needed; physical capital alone cannot ensure either wealth or happiness. Modern knowledge economies require a highly skilled workforce, not just an elite, since economic growth is driven by a powerful interaction between increased human competence and the adoption of new technology. Individuals need high-level skills as well since, without them, they are at great risk of exclusion.[9]

Educational improvements must carry through all twelve years of preparatory education. Kati Haycock, director of the Education Trust, which lobbies on behalf of underprivileged children, writes, "Almost all our reform energy has focused on elementary schools. High schools are the most stagnant part of our education system, followed by middle schools."[10]

Strategies to Improve Education in America

What workable strategies could stop this decline and reverse it?

Accountability

Accountability is the primary prerequisite for improvement. Accountability in education takes the form of standardized tests and numbers of successful graduates. How are you going to know if you are succeeding in meeting your educational goals unless you measure the results? Even in playing football, you measure every play. ("You got two yards on this carry." "This pass was for ten yards and you got a first down." "You got sacked and you lost ten yards.") You need some means of measurement in order to know whether you are advancing or not.

Testing measures achievement, and it becomes the basis by which we can set goals. Test results also become the basis by which we reward (or correct) teachers and administrators, whose job is to make sure the children are getting well educated. If tests show that the children are not getting what they need and the school is not doing something about it, I say let the children go somewhere else to find better education. That's just common sense to me.

We also need clearer accountability via student educational reports. The public education system seems to be doing all it can do to hide the facts from the parents. Too often, when parents get a report about their child, it isn't in plain language, so they don't know what the system actually produced. They don't know how their child is doing. I believe that all school reports should use plain language that someone with an eighth-grade education could comprehend.

Many efforts to achieve better accountability have been tried, and others are in the works. The 2002 federal law known as the No Child Left Behind Act seems to be fueling higher achievement, particularly among the poor and minorities in urban areas, by holding schools accountable for academic progress. Entire school systems, such as the one in Norfolk, Virginia, which was recently awarded the prestigious Broad Prize for Urban Education, have made consistent, measurable academic progress.[11] All of the nearly fifty schools in the system test their students at least four times a year, with some adding weekly or monthly assessments. Groups of teachers evaluate test results in great detail in order to determine educational weak spots. One goal is to troubleshoot *before* the end of the year, when it's too late to help low-performing students. With frequent evaluation, teaching and learning grow and improve hand in hand, as they should.

Accountability that is only test-based is not adequate if it does not sufficiently reward and motivate the very ones who implement its strategies, the teachers and school officials. For too many years, we have made efforts to improve the quality of American education while mollifying the guardians of the failing system, namely educational bureaucrats and teachers unions. This is not the way the educational system should be operating in the country that is the leader of the Western world. Successful schools hold their staffs responsible for class performance, and the accountability in those schools includes a built-in system for taking teachers to the next level of excellence.

Noah Rogers, the principal of Lake Taylor High School in Norfolk (a school formerly described by a city councilman as a "dumping ground" for difficult teens), has implemented changes that have improved not only test scores but also other measures of excellence such as higher attendance, lower dropout rate, and improved discipline. He revamped the curriculum, lengthened school hours, enforced attendance policies, and offered continual teacher training, and he has gotten results. His school is now sending kids to first-rate colleges. He says, "The message I've got for these kids is, 'If you're poor, it doesn't matter anymore. If you've got the smarts, you're going places.' We are proof that change is possible."[12] Improvement can come with the right ingredients—reliance on state standards and assessments, strong leadership, and a cohesive and clear plan of action.

Competition

Lack of competition breeds mediocrity. Common sense tells you that if you start some enterprise—let's say a shoe store—and you have no competitors, you have no reason to keep up your quality or to increase your business by lowering your prices. The only thing that will motivate you to improve the quality of the shoes you sell or to lower the prices on them is the threat of losing your customers. If the product you sell is inferior, your customers are going to go to the stores that sell better shoes than you do for the same price.

Educational "shoppers" do the same thing. If the quality of the product is missing, the parents who can do so are going to take their children elsewhere. They will enroll their children in private schools, and they will essentially pay twice for their education—once in the form of public school taxes and again in the form of tuition. In spite of the fact that this creates an economic hardship, it's a good thing for schools. It represents healthy competition. The more the administration of a bad school is threatened with an exodus of students, the more quickly they will find some way to improve.

Portability

Parents should be free to choose where to send their children to school. This liberty is of particular importance to minorities, who may have more reasons to want to flee public schools with low ratings. I want the American educational system to make it feasible for parents to move their children to any school in America—and for the money to follow the kid. Make the kid portable, and make the money portable with the kid.

School vouchers, ruled legal by the Supreme Court but disallowed by popular vote in some states, including Michigan, have turned out to be slow to catch on. I would strongly support school vouchers wherever they can be implemented, although I respect the will of the voters. When a school voucher system cannot be implemented, I support any alternative, such as tax credits, that can help to provide legitimate educational choices for parents. In Michigan and in thirty-nine other states, one viable alternative has turned out to be charter schools. (Charter schools are essentially independent public schools that are governed by the same basic rules as traditional public schools, operating under a performance contract known as a "charter." They are founded and maintained by committed educators who want to provide an alternative to other public schools.)

In brief, if you have the option of leaving a school system, that system becomes subject to the checks and balances of a free market, which is one of the most important verities of American life. Portability and choice will introduce healthy competition and raise standards across the board.

Teacher specialists

As quickly as possible, I believe that we should identify the topics of study that are falling behind and recruit experts in those fields to teach, full or part time. Granted, there are experts in any field who cannot teach well at all. But most people who have mastered their subject matter could do a good job with only a minimal amount of teacher-training.

I am reminded of a situation in the chemistry department of a local school. A high school chemistry teacher happened to be in a car accident. While she recovered, the school district sent a series of substitute teachers to the class. The kids had been having a bad year to start with, because their original teacher was not a very inspiring one, and now it got worse. Because chemistry was not their forte, most of the substitutes didn't stay long. Then along came Mr. Prudhomme, a retired chemist who happened to be the grandfather of one of the students. He filled in for the disabled teacher for months, and the kids flourished. In fact, for many of them, his teaching provided the first positive experience of a science class that they had ever had. If Mr. Prudhomme could have hired on as a full-time teacher in this public school, the story could have had an even better ending.

Immigration

In our institutions of higher education, we should make it easier for internationals to become students, teachers, or researchers. This has become a bigger issue than it was before 9/11, because now homeland security concerns make it more difficult for foreign students to obtain the appropriate visas. International enrollment has gone down markedly. This may well have the effect of further eroding our competitive edge. We need to employ tight national security, but we shouldn't make the process of obtaining a visa so burdensome that we turn away the bright teachers and students who want to enroll in American colleges. Other countries used to lament the "brain drain" to America. Today, the brightest brains are staying home.

Rewarding Improvement

We should act as quickly as possible to stem the receding educational tide. Time is of the essence. We are over-supplied with wisdom from educational surveys and studies that explain in flowing language and elaborate charts what basic common sense has already told us—the American school system is in trouble, and somebody needs to fix it.

Education is supposed to be, first and foremost, for educating kids, not for providing secure jobs for administrators and educational professionals. I happen to believe that you get more of what you reward and less of what you punish. So we should reward administrators and teachers with higher pay if they can turn out students with higher scores. At the present time, we have this backward. We pay an inordinate amount of attention to taking care of the educational professionals, and we point the finger somewhere else when the kids can't perform well. I advocate local control over schools.

Priority = Kids

Education should be about kids. These kids are going to grow up and take their place in society. American industry, which is increasingly technology-driven and computer-regulated, needs educated employees. Our military must have bright, well-trained minds. Even to do a factory job, a person needs to be literate and well trained.

We cannot fail to educate our kids well. We cannot sit by while higher education slips. We cannot afford to pay such a steep price over the long haul.

CHAPTER 8

COMMONSENSE LEGAL REFORM

WE LIVE IN THE MOST LITIGIOUS SOCIETY IN THE WORLD. IRONICALLY, THIS IS MAKING US LESS FREE THAN WE USED TO BE. IT APPEARS THAT THE GREAT EFFORT TO PROTECT AND ENHANCE OUR SO-CALLED "RIGHTS" IS HAVING THE OPPOSITE EFFECT ON OUR BASIC RIGHTS TO LIFE, LIBERTY, AND THE PURSUIT OF HAPPINESS.

Some of the lawsuits are ridiculous. Remember the notorious woman in Albuquerque who sued McDonald's for making their coffee too hot? (She won, and then the case was appealed, which resulted in a confidential but probably still substantial settlement.) Then there are the

lawsuit-deterring warning labels on products you purchase. Your new baby stroller comes with a precaution-
ary notice: "Please remove child before closing stroller."
Just in case you didn't know.

Those reports may provide comic relief, but it's not so
funny anymore if you lose your job when your employer
goes bankrupt because of a spurious class-action suit.
Nobody laughs when medical bills skyrocket because
of the high cost of malpractice insurance. What's going
on, anyway?

This preoccupation with our almighty rights didn't
always characterize Americans. The prevailing "right"
for most of the history of the nation was simply the commonsense right to be left alone, which made all the fuss
unnecessary.

Now look at the bloated dockets throughout our
court system, not to mention the time and money that's
been wasted and the general disdain of the public for
the legal profession. It's time for the federal government
to do something. The blight extends all the way up to
the most important court of the land.

The Supreme Court

The Supreme Court consists of one chief justice and
eight associate justices, who are, as we have recently
observed in action, appointed by the president and
approved by the Senate. Out of proportion to its size
and historical clout, the Supreme Court in the past few
decades has been accorded an unparalleled prominence,

largely because of an ongoing number of controversial decisions that have revealed a marked tendency of the Court to "legislate from the bench."

It's important to review the fact that the Court doesn't exist to originate laws. This may be news to some people. Many otherwise well-informed citizens believe that, because the Court seems to have the infallible "final word" in all matters it chooses to take up, its opinions are superior to the laws of the land. In the public perception and even sometimes in the lower courts, the Court's word tends to acquire an unalterable forcefulness.

Originating federal laws is the job of the elected members of Congress. The Supreme Court has a different purpose. It was established by the U.S. Constitution to provide balance by interpreting the laws and decisions that are already on the books. The Court reviews both federal and state laws, the opinions of lower courts, and the actions of federal and state executives, and it issues its own opinions, especially where constitutionality is concerned.

The decisions of the Supreme Court are final in that they may not be further appealed. Although the Court does not have an enforcement arm, compliance for its decisions is generally obtained through an unwritten code of respect.

The Founding Fathers never intended for this handful of judges to take on a legislative role. Thomas Jefferson agreed with the others that decisions by the

Supreme Court are simply opinions, and they carry no force of law. In Jefferson's view:

> [T]o consider the judges as the ultimate arbiters of all constitutional questions [is] a very dangerous doctrine indeed, and one which would place us under the despotism of an oligarchy....The Constitution has erected no such single tribunal.[1]

Today's skewed perception developed gradually so that most people didn't notice, although astute observers could recognize the makings of a problem. Even Jefferson expressed some trepidation about the potential for dominance in the judicial branch of the United States government:

> [T]he federal judiciary...work[s] like gravity by night and by day, gaining a little today and a little tomorrow, and advancing its noiseless step like a thief over the field of jurisdiction until all shall be usurped.[2]

Did you realize that Supreme Court decisions can be superseded or disputed in other forums—or even ignored? That's what Abraham Lincoln and the Republicans did when the Supreme Court, dominated by proslavery Democrats, handed down the *Dred Scott v. Sandford* decision in 1857. He disagreed so strongly with the words of the decision—which declared that blacks were not persons or citizens, but merely property that could be bought and sold, with no civil rights—that he

ran for president in 1860. Northern Democrat Stephen
A. Douglas, his opponent, attacked Lincoln because of
this position:

> Mr. Lincoln goes for a warfare upon the Supreme
> Court of the United States, because of their
> judicial decision in the Dred Scott case. I yield
> obedience to the decisions in that court—to the
> final determination of the highest judicial tribunal
> known to our constitution.[3]

As we know, Abraham Lincoln won that election.
Upon his inauguration as president, he and the new
Republican majority in Congress began to dismantle
the slavery machine piece by piece. The process was
so contentious that it led to the Civil War between the
northern and southern states. The *Dred Scott* decision
did not prevail. Instead, the Thirteenth, Fourteenth,
and Fifteenth amendments to the Constitution were
established to protect civil rights.

The *Roe v. Wade* decision of 1973 has assumed a
similar significance in our day. Whereas in *Dred Scott v.
Sandford* constitutionally guaranteed civil rights were
denied to blacks, in *Roe v. Wade* they have been denied
to unborn babies. In both cases, the Court that handed
down the decision was dominated by justices who held
a particular opinion.

President Bush referenced the connection between
these two cases during the second Bush-Kerry debate
on October 8, 2004. The question on the floor was how

the president would handle a Supreme Court vacancy. He responded to indicate that he does not favor activist judges who legislate from the bench, but rather constructionist judges who adhere to the meaning and intent of the Constitution of the United States:

> Another example would be the *Dred Scott* case, which is where judges, years ago, said that the Constitution allowed slavery because of personal property rights. That's a personal opinion. That's not what the Constitution says. I would pick people [for the Supreme Court] that would be strict constructionists. We've got plenty of lawmakers in Washington, D.C. Legislators make the law, judges interpret the Constitution. No litmus tests except for how they interpret the Constitution.[4]

Today, the so-called "balance of power" between the legislative, executive, and judicial branches of the federal government isn't very balanced. It has tilted in the direction of the Court. The justices, because they are appointed for life and cannot be removed from office except by impeachment, seem to be able to operate with impunity.

However, the American people do have a voice. They are free to express their opinions of Court opinions. They are actually free to exert pressure, directly or indirectly through their elected representatives in Congress, on the justices. The true judicial and legislative power belongs, as it always has, to the people, through their exercise of free speech, the casting of their votes for elected legislators, their support of legislative measures that would limit judicial power, and even their involvement in the trial-by-jury process in the lower courts.

The late Chief Justice William Rehnquist summarized the historical view:

> The founders of our Nation considered the right of trial by jury in civil cases an important bulwark against tyranny...a safeguard too precious to be left to the whim of...the judiciary....Trial by a jury of laymen rather than by the sovereign's judges was important to the founders because juries represent the laymen's common sense...and thus keeps the administration of law in accord with the wishes and feelings of the community.[5]

In case it is ever needed, the Constitution also includes a provision for the impeachment of Supreme Court justices.[6] Impeachable offenses include, of course, "treason, bribery, or other high crimes and misdemeanors."[7] Article III, Section 1, Paragraph 1 contains what is known as the "good behavior" clause: "The Judges, both of the Supreme and inferior Courts, shall hold their offices during good behavior." As a protection against abuse, the impeachment provision requires the confirmation of a two-thirds vote of the Senate, which can be a difficult margin to attain. Over the history of the republic, no Supreme Court justice has ever been removed from office, although many have resigned for a variety of reasons.

Don't get me wrong here—I'm not advocating the actual removal of particular Supreme Court justices. However, I would like to raise the visibility of the impeachment option in order to increase the accountability factor. We have a situation where the givens are as follows: (1) Supreme Court justices are appointed for life. (2) They do not have to answer to an electorate. (3) Their day-to-day duties, including details of the case-hearing process, are conducted away from the public eye, for the most part. Therefore, it's easy to see how activist justices can exert their judicial power in the form of legislative power, delivering authoritative decisions that have no reference point in the Constitution. They need to be held accountable.

Because both liberals and conservatives have a big investment in what happens within the court chambers, the Supreme Court does come under very close scrutiny these days. I believe that is a good thing. Like President Bush and many others, I support strict constructionist judges. Judges should interpret the letter of the law and not use it as a tool of legislative reform for their particular special interest groups.

Tort Reform

What is a "tort" anyway? Broadly speaking, it is simply a legal wrong. Laws that concern torts are civil laws (not contract or property laws), where the disagreement is typically, although not exclusively, between private parties. The plaintiff is the victim of the alleged wrong-doing, and the defendant is the one who is accused of perpetrating the wrong. A successful plaintiff receives a payment of damages from the defendant, or, at the least, the defendant is directed to desist from the harmful activity. "Intentional torts" include battery, defamation, and invasion of privacy. "Unintentional torts" include negligence, which can be difficult to assess strictly.

"Tort reform" is a catch-all term, and it can apply to any of the legal reform issues I am addressing in the next part of this chapter. I recognize that tort reform is not on the public's top ten list of burning issues. It's complicated. If you don't feel it has touched you personally, you may decide, understandably, to ignore it. However, you probably cannot ignore it for long, especially if you step into the center ring of public service.

Class actions

Have you ever received an unexpected letter offering you a role in a class-action lawsuit if you will sign on the dotted line? You may have received a "settlement" in one of those cases—in the form of a low-value calling card or a check for a few dollars. What is this all about?

You have brushed up against the epidemic of class-action suits, in which a large number of plaintiffs band together to sue an entity such as a company. If you are my age or older, you will realize that this proliferation of class-action suits is a relatively recent development. Forty years ago, the legal system stayed within certain boundaries. People knew that the terms of their contracts would be enforced and that their basic rights would be protected. Then something happened. Personal injury lawyers began to exploit grievances and eventually to advertise their services, sometimes banding together into firms that specialized in personal injury class-action lawsuits.

Unspoken assumptions changed. Much too often, predatory attorneys who stood to profit handsomely from someone's misfortune filed frivolous lawsuits. The victim or victims did not receive much of a windfall in most cases, and the party who was the object of the suit often lost his livelihood. Businesses were decimated. Only one result was guaranteed: each costly affair would line the pockets of the legal team who staged the action. To ensure the biggest settlements, lawyers shopped around to find a sympathetic judge. Some courts developed a reputation as class-action hot spots.

Often companies pursued by class-action lawsuits have had no recourse except bankruptcy. Companies on the sidelines look on nervously, lest they be next. The litigious atmosphere is inhospitable to domestic job creation and business growth investment. In fact, one of the benefits of setting up shop overseas is that such a company does not have to keep looking over its shoulders for the next antagonistic tort action; it has escaped the legal bloodhounds.

In February of 2005, President Bush signed into law the Class-Action Fairness Act, which received wide bipartisan support in both houses of Congress. Now we will see if this rampant misuse of legal power can be resolved. As the president pointed out at the signing ceremony:

> Class-actions can serve a valuable purpose in our legal system. They allow numerous victims of the same wrong-doing to merge their claims into a single lawsuit. When used properly, class-actions make the legal system more efficient and help guarantee that injured people receive proper compensation. That is an important principle of justice. So the bill I sign today maintains every victim's right to seek justice, and ensures that wrong-doers are held to account.

The bill also disallowed "venue shopping." Hopefully the bill will make it a thing of the past for lawyers to seek out sympathetic judges. About this, the president went on to say:

> Class-actions can also be manipulated for personal gain. Lawyers who represent plaintiffs from multiple states can shop around for the state court where they expect to win the most money. A few weeks ago, I visited Madison County, Illinois, where juries have earned a reputation for awarding large verdicts. The number of class-actions filed in Madison County has gone from two in 1998 to 82 in 2004—even

though the vast majority of the defendants named in those suits are not from Madison County. Trial lawyers...filed...20 [class-actions in Madison County]...in the past week—after Congress made it clear their chance to exploit the class-action system would soon be gone.[8]

Class-action lawsuits need to have their tarnished reputation restored. They should be a legitimate recourse for people who have suffered valid harm. But class-action suits should be formed only by the aggrieved parties themselves, not by greedy law firms. Frivolous class-action suits should become a thing of the past, a temporary trend that comes to a well-deserved demise.

Litigious America

Beyond class-action suits, all of litigious America needs reform. We see advertising for legal services everywhere, on every form of media: television, radio, magazines and newspapers, billboards, the Internet. I am not alone in my opinion that there are way too many ambulance-chasing lawyers on the loose, not to mention fat cat corporate and defense lawyers. They are giving the legal profession a bad rap.

The United States has the dubious distinction of having the highest litigation costs per person in the industrialized world. This cost is not invisible. Small businesses, for example, spend an average of $150,000 per year on legal expenses.[9] Costs of lawsuits, even less frivolous ones, end up paying the fees of the lawyers instead of becoming part of the awards to injured parties. Instead of remaining the protectors of civil justice, members of the law profession as well as ordinary citizens have started to act like piranhas, with a taste for bloody legal disputes.

As my friend Newt Gingrich puts it succinctly in his book *Winning the Future*:

> Laws are being changed from an instrument of justice into an instrument of revenge and redistribution. Americans are learning to treat litigation as a lottery, to sue rather than settle, and to turn American civil life into one of conflict and suspicion.[10]

We are all harmed when people get multimillion-dollar settlements for issues that should have resulted in judgments of $50,000. We all pay for it. The legal profession should not be allowed to rape, plunder, and pillage the way they do, taking a huge percentage of settlements and leaving victims with 25 percent or less—whatever the jury award turns out to be. Injured parties should be guaranteed at least 85 percent of a settlement, with no more than 15 percent going to the personal injury lawyers—with mandatory public disclosure so that fees don't rise to unreasonable levels to make up the difference.

Personal injury lawyers, when they bring cases without merit, should be required to pay court costs, and plaintiffs who bring cases without substance should be docked for court costs, which should be doubled or tripled as a penalty.

Personal injury lawyers should be banned (as they used to be) from advertising. Lawsuits should not be commercialized or foisted on unwary citizens who, bombarded with frequent reminders about their right to feel outraged and to sue, are not only being deprived of an environment of a mature response to difficulties, but are also being led to believe that all lawyers are sharks.

Lastly, simple arbitration, which is cheaper and less rancorous than full-fledged litigation, should be preferred as a means of settling grievances and disputes.

Medical liability reform

All over the United States, medical malpractice insurance costs are crippling physicians, particularly obstetricians and neurosurgeons. Some of them have been forced to close their practices, move to other states, or switch to another field of practice. Small communities, which desperately need medical facilities, suffer the most when this happens.

Unfortunately also, research, development, and merchandising of new drugs are limited because of the threat of lawsuits. Drug companies cannot afford to develop the specialized drugs that are needed to treat rare diseases because tort liability will certainly outweigh investment returns. They end up supporting their research and development programs by charging

Americans 30 percent higher prices for their drugs than they charge the rest of the world. The patients who need the drugs pay the highest price—both in terms of costs and in terms of quality of health care.

Federal legislation to cap escalating malpractice awards might help to address part of the problem. What we need is commonsense medical liability reform that will:

- Protect patients

- Cap the skyrocketing costs that stem from malpractice insurance

- Enable more Americans to afford appropriate medical care

- Keep medical facilities from going under because of costs

Association Health Plans (AHPs)

For five years, health insurance premiums have been growing by an average rate that is more than five times the rate of inflation. This hits small businesses hard. Lacking the market leverage of big companies, small businesses occupy a weaker position in terms of their ability to pool risk and obtain affordable health-care plans for their employees.

The United States Small Business Administration's Office of Advocacy released a report in August 2005 that details the cost of employee benefits by firm size.[11] The report includes the following points:

- In the smallest firms, fewer than 40 percent of the employees are eligible for coverage by health insurance. This is contrasted to the largest firms, in which more than 77 percent of the employees are eligible for health coverage. Conclusion: Firm size affects the ability of an employer to offer benefits.

- From the mid-1990s until 2002, small companies experienced a more rapid rise in health insurance premiums than did bigger companies. Companies that had less than ten employees experienced a weighted average premium that rose 63.2 percent in that time period.

- For small companies, the administrative costs are as much as fourteen times what they are for larger companies.

The U.S. House has already passed a version of an Association Health Plans act. The Small Business Health Fairness Act of 2005 (S.406) is receiving much support in the Senate. Once AHP proposals pass in both houses of Congress, relief will be at hand for owners of small businesses across the nation. They will be able to band together to obtain benefits for their employees that are not only more affordable to the company but also better for the employees.

Asbestos tort litigation

Asbestos tort litigation has almost become synonymous with bankruptcy, having resulted in the bankruptcies of at least seventy-four companies as of this writing. In Michigan alone, asbestos tort litigation has put tens of thousands of citizens out of work.

Asbestos itself is a natural substance that has been used by people for centuries. In the industrialized world, it is used in countless consumer, industrial, maritime, scientific, building, and automotive applications, including brake and clutch assemblies. Prolonged exposure to inhaling asbestos fibers can cause lung diseases, asbestosis, lung cancer, and mesothelioma, which is a form of cancer. In spite of widespread limitations on the use of asbestos since the 1970s, it is required for many manufacturing purposes, and preexisting installations in buildings remain legal.

Federal-Mogul, an auto supplier based in my community of Southfield, Michigan, was forced to file for bankruptcy in 2001. Federal-Mogul happened to have purchased several companies that had asbestos claims against them already, and by 2001 it was faced with more than 365,000 lawsuits altogether.[12] I cite the company only as an example of the impact of class-action suits specific to asbestos-related illnesses (and lately silica-related ones).

Throughout the nation, more than 8,400 entities have been named as defendants in asbestos-related cases, and more than 730,000 people have filed asbestos-related claims. Asbestos litigation has hit over 90 percent of all American industries, and the cost to businesses and insurance companies has exceeded $70 billion.[13] The litigation has dragged on and on, taking on new forms as time goes on. A study released in May 2005, sponsored by the RAND Institute for Civil Justice, notes that an increasing number—up to 90 percent—of new claims are being filed by plaintiffs who are not sick, but who are claiming remuneration for *potential* asbestos-related sicknesses.[14]

Silica, also known as quartz, is another natural substance that is widely used in industry. Workers who inhale particulate silica can develop silicosis, bronchitis, tuberculosis, autoimmune diseases, and fibrosis of the lungs. The similarities between asbestos and silica in terms of lung damage have led to an increase in asbestos-type cases involving silica. The suspicion is that lawyers are worried that asbestos claims will dry up, and, in part also because of the long latency period before the development of silica-exposure symptoms, silica claims have become the next frontier. In addition, some lawyers have been accused of double-dipping—filing claims from the same set of people for both asbestos and silica exposure (which could rarely happen).

Claims that are potentially fraudulent for other reasons have also been investigated. In June 2005, a U.S. district judge threw out 10,000 silicosis diagnoses on the grounds that the diagnoses were "manufactured" and inadmissible in court.[15] In September 2005, the Manville Personal Injury Settlement Trust, which was established to provide compensation for asbestos victims, blacklisted nine doctors and three X-ray screening companies that had been used in a suspiciously large number of claims submitted to the trust.[16]

Normally, workers who are injured on the job receive compensation through their state's worker compensation programs (which prohibit court action). But in the case of asbestos claims, workers have sued third parties, the companies that made asbestos-containing products, and the often-lucrative cases have snowballed. What has happened is that many of the original companies were forced out of business, so lawyers began to target other companies, such as those who had purchased the original companies. Groups of lawyers assembled potential claimants through the use of heavy Internet and television advertising.

The actual (not potential) victims of diseases related to asbestos exposure do deserve a fair compensatory settlement. There are true victims, people whose working lives have exposed them to so much asbestos that they suffer from debilitating, eventually fatal diseases.

Congress has tried many times to exercise federal oversight and curb the proliferation of asbestos/silica claims, so far without success. Trust funds might seem to be a viable solution, but for businesses, they could prove to be a nightmare situation in which the already struggling companies would be forced to contribute to the trust funds for decades. Most legislators and consultants do agree that a way should be found to limit the filing of lawsuits to people who are actually already ill from their exposure to the substance, although it would be difficult to ascertain who is "sick enough" to sue.

Asbestos tort litigation, along with other aspects of our out-of-control legal system, is a major issue that does not appear to be going away very soon.

CHAPTER 9

DEVELOPING ENERGY RESOURCES

A LOT OF HUMAN ENERGY GOES INTO ARGUING ABOUT ENERGY. WHETHER THE TOPIC IS OIL OR NUCLEAR POWER OR ALTERNATIVE FUELS, THE DISCUSSION ITSELF CAN GENERATE QUITE A BIT OF HEAT. WILDERNESS PRESERVATIONISTS ALWAYS SEEM TO BE CAST IN OPPOSITION TO PROPONENTS OF ECONOMIC DEVELOPMENT, THE RADICAL ENVIRONMENTALISTS AGAINST THE OIL INDUSTRY, THE DEMOCRATS AGAINST THE REPUBLICANS, THE LIBERALS VERSUS THE CONSERVATIVES.

It is my firm conviction (thanks in part to the aggressive debate over the past few decades) that natural resources such as oil and gas can be harvested constructively without damage to the surrounding natural environment.

The Arctic National Wildlife Refuge

Over the past few decades, some of the most rancorous debate has concerned the Arctic National Wildlife Refuge, known by the acronym ANWR. For decades and up to the present time, both houses of Congress have jockeyed back and forth with proposals to permit and fund drilling for oil and natural gas in ANWR. I believe it is educational to examine the details of the argument, because misconceptions have taken root in people's minds. ANWR remains an important component of any discussion about meeting our national energy needs.

In urging Congress to authorize exploration for ANWR oil, President Bush stated that oil could be recovered "with almost no impact on land and local wildlife" and that the production capacity of the oil field would match almost half of what the United States now imports from Venezuela. I believe that these significant claims can be supported from the facts.

I have always been in favor of drilling in ANWR. But this has not been my knee-jerk Republican response to a situation that is remote from my personal experience. Alaska, especially arctic coastal plain that is under scrutiny, may be remote geographically from anyone who is reading this book, but the cost of a barrel of oil has an impact on your daily life as well as my own, even more so because I represent the Motor City, Detroit, where fuel issues are paramount. And Michigan too has untapped oil reserves, concerning which I have a passionate—and the opposite—response. (More about that later.)

I have always wanted to open ANWR to oil and gas exploration and, assuming predictions of abundant oil prove to be true, to allow drilling. But I would always want us to drill responsibly. Given the giant strides that have been made in the past couple of decades toward understanding how to protect the environment while extracting its resources, I believe it can be done without harming wildlife or the ecological balance of the delicate tundra wilderness.

At this point, technological improvements will enable ANWR drilling to represent a very small "footprint" on the land, compared to the successful drilling at nearby Prudhoe Bay, west of the refuge, from which, for the past twenty-eight years, more than fourteen billion barrels of oil have flowed down the Trans-Alaska Pipeline System to the lower forty-eight states. If Prudhoe Bay were built today, the footprint would be 1,526 acres, 64 percent smaller. Technological improvements have increased well productivity, which would mean that fewer oil wells would be required. Improvements have also reduced the size of drilling pads and have made it possible to drill to greater depths, as well as horizontally. In addition, technological advances have reduced the costs of monitoring and transporting the product over long distances.

The proposal for the Alaska pipeline aroused environmental concerns in the late 1960s and early 1970s. The concerns were taken into consideration, and, even without the current level of technological development, the impact on wildlife and human beings has been quantifiably positive. Energy development and wildlife are coexisting with success throughout the region affected by the Prudhoe Bay oil fields. In fact, the caribou herd that migrates through that area has grown from 3,000 in 1977 to a current estimated level of 23,400 animals.[1] The area is also home to a healthy population of brown bears, foxes, and birds that parallels the count in adjacent areas. Other species include polar bears, musk oxen, and over a hundred species of migratory birds.

From the economic point of view, the existing Alaskan pipeline has been a boon to the state of Alaska and beyond, bringing in between $50 and $69 billion in revenue and creating tens of thousands of jobs. The construction of the pipeline alone (1969–1977) created 70,000 jobs.[2]

Parenthetically, we should note that drilling in Alaska represents a much safer situation than drilling, for instance, underwater in the Gulf of Mexico (from which we obtain almost 28 percent of our oil at present). Witness the destruction to oil rigs and disruption of oil shipments that resulted from hurricanes Katrina and Rita—with the ongoing threat of more extreme storms in the future.

Alaskan oil is drilled and shipped on solid ground, under a set of environmental regulations that is unrivaled on the face of the earth. Oil has been flowing from Prudhoe Bay for almost thirty years with only the occasional spill. In spite of the inhospitable climate, there has been relatively little interference with the flow because of natural disasters or weather. That's a pretty good record, and it can be improved if ANWR oil is extracted and shipped.

Something like 88 percent of the fuel for industry, transportation, and residential needs in the United States is derived from oil, gas, and coal. We must continue to develop fossil fuels while we also develop alternative energy sources—but we cannot cut off fossil fuels prematurely.

Size of ANWR

The Arctic National Wildlife Refuge covers 19 million acres of arctic wilderness in northeastern Alaska—an area roughly the same size as the state of South Carolina—on the Beaufort Sea. Management of the property is administered by the United States Fish and Wildlife Service, which is part of the Department of the Interior. It is a treeless, arctic landscape, tundra, mountains, and—of primary interest to oil industry developers—a 1.5 million-acre coastal plain.

In the region around the refuge are scattered villages inhabited by natives who identify themselves as either Gwich'in or Inupiat Eskimo. The Gwich'in tribe, although they have switched sides on the question, presently hold the view that drilling is a threat to their caribou-based subsistence lifestyle. The Inupiat, who have benefited economically from the existing oil industry, favor further development.

Proposed drilling acreage

The geologists and scientists from other disciplines who have conducted extensive studies of the area have agreed (regardless of their political persuasion) that the coastal plain of ANWR is also an oil refuge of the highest onshore magnitude yet to be investigated on the North American continent, probably rivaling the nearby Prudhoe Bay oil field.

However, of the total of 19 million acres, 17.16 million acres are protected by law against all development; they are to remain a wilderness refuge. Less than 2,000 acres of the coastal plain, or 3.13 square miles (which is only .0001 percent—one hundredth of one percent—of the entire acreage of ANWR) will be developed.

Caribou, other wildlife, and the environment

Vast amounts of research on wildlife and arctic ecosystems have been conducted on Alaska's North Slope (Prudhoe Bay and surroundings). As a result, we know that the best possible coexistence between wildlife and oil development is not only feasible but is already demonstrable. Oil field construction has been undertaken with wildlife in mind, and it has disrupted a minimal amount of tundra surface.

Based on the existing oil field and pipeline, it

appears that adult male caribou adjust easily to evidences of human presence, sometimes even seeking out the gravel pads or pipeline roads, where heavy insect attacks appear to be lighter. Females prefer to avoid human installations during calving season, and this would provide more concern in ANWR than in the Prudhoe Bay area, because the habitat range is more restricted. However, calving studies have been conducted since 1983, and not once in more than twenty years has the proposed ANWR coastal plain drilling area been the females' primary site for calving.

In any case, the regulatory process for obtaining drilling permits has become quite complex and highly protective of the environment since the late 1960s. In ANWR, drilling activity would only take place during the winter months, when caribou do not frequent the coastal plain area.

Economic considerations

Economically speaking, it makes sense to diversify our energy supply. Price spikes, fuel shortages, and other energy uncertainties can be avoided if we don't put all of our energy eggs in a few geographical baskets. The production capacity of the Prudhoe Bay oil field is declining. It only makes sense to drill new wells in the nearby region in order to maintain the supply that can come from the far north.

A parallel economic consideration is job creation. Whenever new development occurs, the American economy benefits through the creation of construction, service, manufacturing, and engineering jobs. Estimates vary widely, but potential jobs directly related to ANWR development (spread across all fifty states) range from 250,000 to 735,000.[3] In addition, the federal government would receive steady revenue in the form of taxes, royalties, bonus bids, and lease rentals.

Future energy needs

The demand for crude oil in the United States can only increase, even if the rate at which it increases slows due to consumption regulations. Rather than relying on imports to meet our energy needs, it would be preferable to rely on our own resources. In 2004, the United States imported an average of 58 percent of its oil, during certain months up to 64 percent. Even if the extraction of ANWR oil is undertaken soon (as well as natural gas, if it becomes economically practical), actual production capacity will not be reached for at least eight years.

The Alaska oil fields at Prudhoe Bay, Kuparuk, Lisburne, and Endicott currently account for about 25 percent of the domestic oil production in the United States. The Gulf of Mexico accounts for 28 percent of domestic oil production. In the past thirty years, no new major discoveries of oil reserves have been made within the country—except in Alaska. With the addition of ANWR development, about 33 percent of our domestic production of oil could come from Alaska, surpassing the output of the weather-vulnerable Gulf of Mexico.

The oil pipeline in Alaska needs to be used to its full capacity. Currently, because of the decline of the output from Prudhoe Bay and vicinity, it carries less than half of what it should. Development of a new oil field will keep it in operation. Without new development, the entire pipeline system faces eventual decommissioning and dismantling.

Protection from spills at sea

The crude oil from the existing oil fields is transported to refineries via the Alaska pipeline to the ice-free port of Valdez in southern Alaska. From there it is shipped to refineries on the West Coast. In 1990, the Oil Pollution Act began to require that as obsolescent tankers are replaced, the new ones must be better designed double-hulled vessels. This provides valuable protection for the waters through which the tankers travel.

For all of these reasons, I believe that tapping into the oil supply in the ANWR coastal plain should not be a matter of further prolonged debate. We need it. It is available. And it can be obtained without harming the environment. It's a no-brainer.

Refineries

Needless to say, even if you have all the oil in the world, it's no good to you if you cannot refine it and convert it to a usable form. The United States has not built a new refinery for thirty years. Why is this? In part because environmental regulations have gone crazy. The rules are so stringent that it has made it unprofitable to build new refineries in America. The other reason is because of the consequences of tax policy. As I mentioned earlier, American businesses pay the highest corporate income taxes in the industrialized world—35 percent. So when you add that to super-stringent environmental regulations, you kill all incentives to build refineries.

True, refineries are not the best neighbors to have. They tend to be sprawling and foul-smelling, and often other undesirable industries locate nearby in order to use their products. So there is always the NIMBY (Not in My Backyard) citizen movement factor as well.

As we have seen all too well in the past year, many of our current refineries lie in the path of dangerous weather patterns. So on top of the basic fact that our refineries are aging and we need more of them, we need to replace some of the ones upon which we have relied. Immediately after Hurricane Katrina, Rep. John Sullivan (R-OK) issued a statement:

> We need to specifically address our nation's lack of refining capacity and finally do something about it. Hurricane Katrina has further underscored the fact that our refining capacity is inadequate.[4]

The Department of Energy reports that the United States had 324 refineries (total capacity: 18.6 million barrels per day) in 1981. Today, due to regulations and consolidations, *Oil and Gas Journal* reports that only

132 refineries remain, with a total capacity of 16.8 million barrels per day.[5]

Opponents of refinery development voice concerns that clean-air laws will be relaxed for the sake of building refineries. Industry proponents argue for tax breaks. Congress is where these debates occur, as policymakers ponder the implications of their decisions.

Like many issues of concern to lawmakers, this one cuts across many related issues, including energy, the environment, and taxes. In my opinion, energy is also a national security issue. I believe a government should make sure that certain things happen. Until we establish some commonsense benchmarks in Congress, we will continue to drown in committees and partisan bickering and red tape.

Michigan and the Great Lakes

I am not saying that I believe the United States should drill for oil wherever it can be found. If it cannot be done safely in a particular location, as is possible in Alaska, I believe drilling should be banned. The Great Lakes provide a good example.

The Great Lakes are well named; they are so immense that they are easy to spot on pictures taken from satellites. They are, from west to east, Lakes Superior, Michigan, Huron, Erie, and Ontario. The lakes are surrounded by the Canadian province of Ontario and eight states of the United States—Minnesota, Wisconsin, Illinois, Indiana, Michigan, Ohio, Pennsylvania, and

New York. Taken as a group, the Great Lakes are the largest surface freshwater reservoir in the world, and the Great Lakes basin is home to 30 million people. The Great Lakes may be vast in size, but they are not invulnerable to human intrusions. The ecosystem they represent is susceptible to disturbances and difficult to repair.

In terms of energy sources, the Great Lakes cover untapped underwater oil fields. Pro-drilling energy companies commonly cite statistics from a 1997 study that showed that drilling would be safe in terms of oil spills and contamination. However, their statistics do not include information about the greater potential for oil and hydrogen sulfide leaks from shoreline wells, which would put fragile coastal ecology and the human population at risk. A lakeshore environment is not resilient. If contamination occurs, environmental balance and health may be permanently lost.

In any case, the amount of retrievable oil that resides under the Great Lakes is relatively small—definitely not worth the risk to the fresh water, to the ecological balance of the region, and to millions of citizens of Great Lakes states. Cam Davis, director of the Alliance for the Great Lakes in Chicago, says:

> The amount of fossil fuel under the Great Lakes is so small that it really wouldn't fuel the country for very long, probably a matter of minutes really. The amount that's down there and the amount it could supply us is not worth the risk.[6]

People themselves are part of the environment that needs to be protected. It seems to me and many others that it is one thing to drill for oil in the middle of a dry western state where the population may be a handful of individuals per square mile, and another to drill under the largest fresh-water reservoir in the world, where 30 million people live.

One by one, many of the states surrounding the Great Lakes have enacted drilling bans, Michigan included, although Indiana, Pennsylvania, and Minnesota have not had drilling bans. Because drilling for oil under any of the five Great Lakes would have regional impact beyond an individual state, the Energy Bill signed into law by President Bush in August 2005 bans drilling under the Great Lakes.

It will be imperative to hold the line on that one.

Other sources of pollution

I mentioned above the double-hulled tankers that are beginning to carry Alaskan crude oil to refineries. Even without actual drilling under the Great Lakes, the waterways are a key shipping network for many goods, including oil. Without question, I favor the use of double-hulled tankers in the Great Lakes.

In addition, I will support legislation that keeps ballast water from other countries from being discharged directly into the lakes. The United States Coast Guard Office of Operating and Environmental Standards declares:

Every day, large quantities of ballast water from all over the world are discharged into United States waters. Carried in this water are plants, animals, bacteria, and pathogens. These organisms range in size from microscopic to large plants and free-swimming fish. These organisms have the potential to become aquatic nuisance species (ANS). ANS may displace native species, degrade native habitats, spread disease, and disrupt human social and economic activities that depend on water resources. Any ship carrying ballast water is a potential invasion source.[7]

The aquatic environments and economies of my state and others around the Great Lakes already have suffered greatly from the accidental introduction of the zebra mussel, whose tiny larvae were apparently transported by ballast water of an ocean-going vessel, ballast water that was taken from a freshwater source in Asia and released in the Detroit area prior to 1988. Besides the zebra mussel, a number of other invasive species of mollusks, crustaceans, fish, and plants have already taken hold. With strict regulations, we can prevent the introduction of others that lack natural predators in the Great Lakes region. I support all research and efforts to eliminate invasive species that have already taken hold, as well as laws that will curtail future incursions. We can't upset the natural balance any further.

We can't pollute the Great Lakes. I'm in favor of federal rules to stop runoff into the Great Lakes. Fish contaminated by industrial waste, beaches closed because of bacteria, and waterways clogged with algae are the legacy of unregulated growth.

In addition, there is risk to the environment and to humans from the nuclear waste that must be stored on-site at two nuclear power plants next to Lake Michigan instead of being shipped to Yucca Mountain in Nevada. The Nuclear Waste Policy Act charged the U.S. Department of Energy (DOE) with finding safe and permanent nuclear waste disposal sites, and Yucca Mountain is the preferred site. However, in spite of the suitability of Yucca Mountain, congressional haggling has postponed the date that the facility will actually begin to accept waste. Meantime, Michigan and other states play the waiting game with an ever-increasing number of barrels of nuclear waste that are temporarily and insecurely stored. In total, the United States has more than 47,500 metric tons of spent nuclear waste that is stored in forty-three states, and by 2040, it is projected that there will be 108,000 metric tons of spent nuclear waste in the country.[8] Long-term, on-site storage is very inefficient, especially when compared to the unparalleled safety of Yucca Mountain. Barrel leaks and other accidents have already occurred and will continue to occur. The materials are also at risk from terrorism, other kinds of social instability, and even the shifting sand dunes adjacent to Lake Michigan where they are kept in my state.[9]

Since the 1970s, much has been done to clean up the Great Lakes, and we cannot afford to let down our vigilance. It is basic common sense to maintain protective rules and regulations over anything that has the potential to upset the fragile balance of the freshwater lake ecosystem. President Bush executed a Presidential Executive Order in 2004 in which the Great Lakes were declared to be a national treasure. He established an interagency task force that has published a current strategy to restore the lakes so that they can again become truly great.

Alternative Fuels

I'm all for the use of every available fuel technology. I believe we should be using nuclear power, for example. We are not living in the 1970s anymore. Nuclear power does not soil the environment. Nuclear power technology today, developed with public safety in mind, is superior to what it used to be. But we need to determine how much regulation is enough and how to release the stranglehold on the industry that over-regulation has created. As it is with oil refineries, the blame is shared with over-taxation. I want to see intelligent development of the industry.

So does President Bush, and so do an increasing number of legislators and executives. Part of the Energy Policy Act of 2005 includes guarantees, incentives, and tax credits to spur the development of as many as six new nuclear plants. With the ever-rising price of natural gas and the concern to limit greenhouse gases, nuclear power generation is looking better all the time.

Ethanol and methanol

Ethanol and methanol are clean, efficient, alternative fuels. Ethanol, or "grain alcohol," has been used for years as the primary fuel for vehicles in Brazil, and a blend of ethanol and gasoline ("gasohol") is available in the United States. Ethanol can be produced from corn and other crops, even from biomass waste, and it has the potential to minimize greenhouse gases. At present, the market pricing and technology development mean that the cost of ethanol is high, but I support the development of new technologies that would reduce its cost and promote its use.

Methanol, or "wood alcohol," can be produced from wood and coal as well as from natural gas. Most of the auto companies have produced prototype vehicles that can burn methanol. It is currently used as a fuel in race cars and has been since 1965. A combination of 85 percent methanol and 15 percent unleaded regular gasoline is called M85, and it can be used as a liquid fuel with the same convenience as regular gasoline. In fact, flexible-fuel vehicles can use methanol or gasoline in any combination. In other words, a flexible-fuel vehicle can burn regular gasoline when methanol fuel is unavailable, without any conversion procedures. If domestic production of methanol were to be expanded, the best production method would involve coal, which is an abundant resource within the nation.

Common sense tells me that if I can get a car that will essentially burn corn or coal, both of which are rich domestic resources, and I can afford both the car and the fuel, I'll buy it and use it. As a legislator, I want to do my part to support sensible initiatives that will stimulate far-reaching economic growth. I would like to make it possible for an alternative fuel industry to develop and thrive, an industry that reaches into farm country and coal country and beyond.

Wind power, solar power, and hydrogen

Alternative fuels include more than ethanol and methanol. We should also utilize more wind power, solar power, and fuel cell technology. Hydrogen is a feasible option for fuel cell applications, in which it reacts with oxygen to create electricity to power an electric motor. The advantage of wind power, solar power, and hydrogen fuel cells is that they are renewable and clean sources of energy, unlike fossil fuels or even alcohol-based fuels (this assumes that the hydrogen is not produced using hydrocarbons). Buses, submarines, high-speed cars, and space rockets already use hydrogen as fuel. Despite popular perceptions of high-explosive tendencies, hydrogen is safe. Richard Tuso, an electrical technician with Daimler-Chrysler, says that accidental hydrogen fires are not particularly dangerous:

> People think of the Hindenberg and hydrogen bombs.... [Because] hydrogen is a very clean fuel, it will ignite easier than gasoline, but the likelihood of it igniting is still slim. If it did ignite, the flame doesn't put out much heat. Gasoline fires usually consume the whole car.... [10]

All alternative fuels require more development before they are commercially viable. Often the fuel "tank" (or reforming device) is so bulky that the vehicle has no room for passengers. In addition, many of the cars have a limited range, especially a problem given the lack of an existing infrastructure for alternative fuel distribution. Besides, it's sort of a chicken-and-egg problem; development itself is inhibited by the small number of vehicles that can use alternative fuels.

However, alternative fuels are essential if the United States wants to get away from having to depend upon the Arab nations, or at least to get to the point that our Arab imports become insignificant to our overall energy needs.

Universal Standards

I believe that we have to modernize and standardize our utilities transmission grids in the United States. The national electrical power grid is an interconnected network of individual power suppliers from state to state. When one supplier has surplus electrical power, it can be sold to another supplier whose customer demand is high. But if the electric companies in each state follow only their differing state standards, they can't patch together as well as they should.

Much has been accomplished since the Great Blackout of August 2003, which is still fresh in our minds in Michigan. Although much had been improved since the big Northeast Blackout of 1965, it wasn't enough to prevent a massive shutdown of electrical power and a cascading number of public services that depend upon electric power. The crisis closed businesses and schools and caused problems with water supply, rail services, air travel, phone service, and financial markets. Coming after the terrorist attacks of 9/11, it raised fears about the vulnerability of the utility system. The blackout covered roughly 9,300 square miles. One hundred power plants in the United States and Canada were disabled during the blackout.

Like our highway system, the national utilities grid is in perpetual need of maintenance and modernization. Besides providing reliable power to residences, schools, and hospitals, we need to ensure that our utilities systems are unsurpassed for the sake of the economy. Business growth will not occur if the quality of the infrastructure is spotty.

Sustainable Development

Although a healthy nation requires a certain amount of federal regulation, I believe that it is a common modern fallacy to over-protect. With everything, we need balance.

Is it reasonable, for instance, to allow 80 percent of our federal forest land in Michigan to go unharvested? Trees are a renewable resource. When you harvest one, you can leave behind seedlings, plant another one, or follow other proven logging policies that keep the long-term picture in mind. Trees will grow back. If you don't harvest any trees, they drop leaves and limbs and eventually die of old age, creating a fire hazard that can destroy the entire forest. To a much, much greater degree than current environment standards will allow, we could be harvesting trees without sacrificing any trees in the long run.

In other words, cutting a tree can be a good thing, not only a bad thing, if it's done responsibly. Trees provide us with an ideal source for lumber for buildings, fiber- and particleboard, furniture, paper, and a source for methanol, to name a few. The lumber industry provides jobs, the tree is used in any number of other industries, jobs are created and sustained—and the forest is reproduced as well.

I would allow harvesting on federal lands. I'd like to see us harvest 50 to 60 percent of the trees in federal forests, with sustained growth built into the agreement. It's worth knowing if a particular forest is populated with some rare species of animal or plant, but I wouldn't let it compromise the use of the land by human beings. It can be done, with balance and care, without sacrificing valuable, nonrenewable resources. We need to utilize the natural wealth that has been given to us as well as protect it. We can do both at the same time.

COUNTERING GLOBAL THREATS

As a nation, Americans do not seem to have grasped that, by default, we are embroiled in a global war. The way we conduct ourselves shows that the gravity of the situation hasn't hit us.

The headlines seem predictable to us: deaths in Iraq, suicide bombings, the plight of refugees in besieged lands, disputes in Washington, anti-war protests. Yet another threat of a subway terrorist attack passes without incident. The barrage of news may have lulled us into complacency. Despite of the horror of 9/11 and all that has happened since then, it's easy to turn a blind eye to a conflict that stays on the other side of the world, for the most part.

And yet, whether we choose to acknowledge it or not, the United States of America is at war—with a number of ruthless enemies. Our country will be at war for the foreseeable future. We actually could lose this war, lose our lives, and lose the future of a free world. We are not as safe as we thought we were.

> Rely on God and devour the Americans, like lions devour their prey. Bury them in the Iraqi graveyard.[1]
>
> —AYMAN AL-ZAWAHIRI

In this war, international conflicts are not isolated from domestic threats. Homeland security is part of the global war on terrorism. This war has many fronts.

Our primary national leaders comprehend the scale and the scope of the danger we are in. Regarding national security, President Bush has declared:

> Defending our nation against its enemies is the first and fundamental commitment of the federal government. Today, that task has changed dramatically. Enemies in the past needed great armies and great industrial capabilities to endanger America. Now, shadowy networks of individuals can bring great chaos and suffering to our shores for less than it costs to purchase a single tank. Terrorists are organized to penetrate open societies and to turn the power of modern technologies against us.
>
> To defeat this threat we must make use of every

tool in our arsenal—military power, better homeland defenses, law enforcement, intelligence, and
vigorous efforts to cut off terrorist financing. The
war against terrorists of global reach is a global
enterprise of uncertain duration. America will help
nations that need our assistance in combating terror. And America will hold to account nations that
are compromised by terror, including those who
harbor terrorists—because the allies of terror are
the enemies of civilization.[2]

Engaging in the Conflict

Our survival as a nation requires fighting on many
fronts at the same time. We need to follow through
on decisions that have been hard-won in Washington,
becoming as committed to implementing them as we
are to giving speeches and staging interviews and taking opinion polls.

As a foundational strategy, we need to "export" the
idea of democratic freedom just as we export manufactured goods. This is integral to the president's strategy
against terrorism. He has said, "If the Middle East grows
in democracy, prosperity, and hope, the terrorist movement will lose its sponsors, lose its recruits, and lose the
festering grievances that keep terrorists in business."[3]

Toward this end, we need to reengage diplomatic
efforts across the globe, promoting American values
of democratic capitalism. Quiet diplomacy will not cut
it. Neither will policies driven by fluctuating American

public opinion polls. We need a new approach to conflicts that have been long in duration and that cannot be separated from the war on terrorism, such as the struggle for dominance between Israel and Palestine. We need to inundate the airwaves with broadcasts that rival the hostile message of *Al-Jazeera, Al-Arabiya*, and others. We need to stand firm as we get out a bold message: terrorism meets its match in freedom.

Defeating such a broad and adaptive enemy network will require a combination of patience, constant pressure, and strongly forged partnerships with allies. We need to persist in disrupting militant conspiracies, destroying their ability to make war—all the while giving citizens of many nations a hopeful alternative to hatred and violence.

In a speech to the National Endowment for Democracy on October 6, 2005, the President outlined his strategy for winning the war on terrorism. He included the following points:[4]

1. We are *preventing terrorist attacks before they occur.* We are reorganizing government for a broad and coordinated homeland defense, reforming intelligence agencies for the difficult task of tracking enemy activity, and acting, along with governments from many countries, to destroy the terrorist networks and incapacitate their leaders. We have prevented terrorist plots and Al-Qaeda

efforts to case targets in the United States. Because of strikes against terrorist leaders and disruption of their plots, the enemy is wounded but still capable of deadly operations around the globe. Our commitment is clear: we will not relent until the organized international terror networks are exposed and broken and their leaders held to account for their acts of murder.

2. We are *denying weapons of mass destruction to outlaw regimes* and their terrorist allies. Working with Great Britain, Pakistan, and other nations, we shut down A. Q. Khan's black-market operation in nuclear technology. Libya abandoned its chemical and nuclear weapons programs, as well as its long-range ballistic missiles. In the last year, America and our partners in the Proliferation Security Initiative have stopped more than a dozen shipments of suspect weapons technology—including equipment for Iran's ballistic missile programs. This progress has reduced the danger, but not removed it. Evil men still work to gain these weapons, and we are working urgently to keep them out of their hands.

3. We are determined to *deny radical groups the support and sanctuary of outlaw regimes.*

State sponsors like Syria and Iran have a long history of collaboration with terrorists—and they deserve no patience from the victims of terror. The United States makes no distinction between those who commit acts of terror and those who support and harbor terrorists, because they are equally guilty of murder.

4. We are *fighting to deny the militants control of any nation.* The United States is fighting beside our Afghan partners against the remnants of the Taliban and its Al-Qaeda allies. We are working with President Musharraf to isolate the militants in Pakistan. We are fighting the terrorists and regime remnants in Iraq who seek to overthrow a democracy, claim a strategic country as a haven of terror, destabilize the Middle East, and strike America and other free nations with ever increasing violence. Our goal is to defeat the terrorists and their allies at the heart of their power—and we are achieving this goal.

5. We are *denying the militants future recruits by advancing democracy and hope across the broader Middle East.* If the region is left to grow in bitterness and misery, while radicals stir the resentments of millions, then that

part of the world will be a source of endless conflict and mounting danger. However, the extremists will be marginalized and their violence ended if the peoples of that region are permitted to choose their own destiny and advance by their own energy and participation as free men and women. America is making this stand in practical ways. We are encouraging our friends in the Middle East, including Egypt and Saudi Arabia, to take the path of reform to strengthen their own societies in the fight against terror by respecting the rights of people. We are standing with dissidents and exiles against oppressive regimes, because we know that the dissidents of today will be the democratic leaders of tomorrow. We are making our case through public diplomacy— stating clearly and confidently our belief in self-determination, religious freedom, and equal rights for women. By standing for the hope and freedom of others, we will make our own freedom more secure.

Compromised Military Strength

We definitely need to get over our reluctance to promote military strength. I am a Ronald Reagan conservative when it comes to national defense. I believe that diplomacy is important, but that it is simply not enough when you are dealing with armed foes.

Our national defense has not yet recovered from the Clinton era. Case in point: President Clinton initiated the measures that made it illegal for the CIA to contract and to work with people who have a criminal record. Doesn't that sound like it might be a smart idea? Not when you recognize that the only way to *do* undercover intelligence work is to fraternize with criminals. The people who hang with the Saddam Husseins or the Osama bin Ladens of the world are not going to be Boy Scouts! Nevertheless, along comes our own government, saying intelligence agents can't associate with their informants. With one stroke of his pen, President Clinton and Congress wiped out half of our intelligence assets.

Predictably, this happened without much notice from the liberal media. During the 1990s, national security expenditures were treated as a mere expense rather than as an investment in the safety of the nation. The report of the 9/11 Commission noted that this approach had a harmful impact on our intelligence services. The report stated:

> [C]uts in national security expenditures at the end of the Cold War led to budget cuts in the national foreign intelligence program from fiscal years 1990 to 1996 and essentially flat budgets from fiscal years 1996 to 2000....These cuts compounded the difficulties of the intelligence agencies.[5]

These days, all you hear from the liberals is censure for the failure of the CIA to accurately determine whether or not Iraq had weapons of mass destruction. They rail about the failure of the CIA to anticipate 9/11. How could they do their job when their ability to do it was erased like a penciled-in budget item by a liberal Congress and White House?

Here we are, trying to work with intelligence capabilities that are probably only about one-third of what we need. Yet in order to thwart terrorism successfully, the United States must have the best intelligence capabilities in the world. Right now, today (if not yesterday), we need linguists, we need specialists in culture and religion, we need CIA support staff who are versed in history and world political systems. We need more agents out in the field on covert operations, and we need good communication between well-developed teams in order to be able to fit together the puzzle pieces of evidence.

The president expresses the importance of our intelligence-gathering system and its integration with other defensive systems:

> Intelligence—and how we use it—is our first line of defense against terrorists and the threat posed by hostile states. Designed around the priority of gathering enormous information about a massive, fixed object—the Soviet bloc—the intelligence community is coping with the challenge of following

a far more complex and elusive set of targets.

We must transform our intelligence capabilities and build new ones to keep pace with the nature of these threats. Intelligence must be appropriately integrated with our defense and law enforcement systems and coordinated with our allies and friends. We need to protect the capabilities we have so that we do not arm our enemies with the knowledge of how best to surprise us. Those who would harm us also seek the benefit of surprise to limit our prevention and response options and to maximize injury.

We must strengthen intelligence warning and analysis to provide integrated threat assessments for national and homeland security. Since the threats inspired by foreign governments and groups may be conducted inside the United States, we must also ensure the proper fusion of information between intelligence and law enforcement.[6]

The best intelligence systems and the best military systems capitalize on technological advances to the highest degree. Including and beyond "smart bombs," we need to maintain an approach that allows us to use the most sophisticated weapons and information systems in the world. Ronald Reagan's Star Wars program capitalized on technology to end the Cold War. Technology should be used to its fullest to force these twenty-first-century enemies to their knees.

In addition to cutting the intelligence budget, the Clinton Administration cut the military budget drastically. We're still trying to catch up from those years. Military procurement takes so long—even the small stuff takes a long time to acquire—that it's no wonder we don't have properly armored Humvees in Iraq. The funding for that was cut by the previous administration. It goes without saying that the technologically advanced equipment required in this kind of warfare is expensive.

It was dangerously shortsighted to cut military spending. We're not talking about a line item in the federal budget—we're talking about an investment in our future.

Worldwide Preparedness

Militarily, even as we fulfill our obligations in Iraq and Afghanistan and keep an eagle eye on rogue nations around the world, we need to be prepared for an inevitable confrontation with China one day. The Chinese are using much of their gross domestic product to build weapons systems and troop strength at an unprecedented rate, including a navy, which they never had before. In ten years, the Chinese navy will match the American navy in size and strength. That means, for one thing, that the United States will not be able to defend the Taiwan Straits and Taiwan. Our military commitments to freedom around the world will be more difficult to fulfill.

We must respond by building our own military at all costs. But with over a billion Chinese and only 300 million of us, we absolutely must have the technological edge as part of our military edge. We need to have adequate sealift capacity. We need to have increased airlift capacity. We must have intelligence on the ground. We must grow the size of our army, navy, and the other branches of our military.

We need to transform our armed services into expeditionary forces that are more quickly deployable. We could do it by following up on President Bush's efforts to dismantle the old Cold War system, which entailed maintaining military bases throughout Europe and using the resulting savings to support forward operating bases in the Middle East, Central Asia, and South Asia.[7] The wider challenges we are facing require a military capability that is adaptable and primed for a war effort with many fronts.

Many of those fronts seem to appear out of nowhere. Peaceniks don't want to believe that preemptive strikes are ever justified. But a number of countries harbor terrorists and covertly develop weapons. Even when they never intend to employ the weapons themselves, they are glad to sell them to others. Among the most dangerous countries in this regard are Iran and North Korea. Iraq was a similar threat before we intervened. These are "rogue nations," and preemptive efforts to contain their activities are justified.

As President Franklin D. Roosevelt stated in one

of his famous fireside chats (he was talking about pre-emptive efforts to keep the seas free from the threat of German submarines in the western Atlantic):

> When you see a rattlesnake poised to strike, you do not wait until he has struck before you crush him.[8]

This is not only basic common sense; it is smart leadership!

Homeland Security

Top-notch intelligence work combined with diplomatic efforts and preemptive military missions are essential for our national security. However, the battles that need to be waged are not always in foreign countries. Sometimes they are in our own states or communities, within our own borders.

I believe that our homeland defense is synonymous with our national security. The attacks on 9/11 proved that, as a nation, we are woefully insecure. We must be able to anticipate and defend our own cities.

We need a homeland security system that can handle any threat. Our current Department of Homeland Security, reorganized as it was from existing departments within the governmental bureaucracy, is not adequate to the task. It needs to be stripped for action, without further encumbrance from political agendas and internal contention. The dangers to the security of our nation are multifaceted; they include nuclear, biological, chemical, and conventional weapons. The same technological advances that can be used for our protection can be used against us—and they will be implemented without regard to human decency. We need to be ready.

Nuclear weapons can be transported secretly across borders. Biological and chemical weapons can cause such widespread disruption that they would inflict damage to the nation comparable to a massive bomb explosion. Electromagnetic pulse (EMP) weapons could be used to bring down the nation's electrical systems. Without electricity, our ability to defend ourselves militarily would be nil.

We have seen the cold malice of the fanatics who are targeting the United States. Their leaders are explicit about their intentions to kill and maim Americans in the name of Allah. Ayman al-Zawahiri, considered to be second in command to Osama bin Laden, said this in one of his taped statements that was released to the Arab press:

> You Bush, protect your country and step up your security measures. The Islamic Ummah Mujaheda (Nation of fighters), which sent its brigades to New York and Washington, is determined to send more Death Brigades.[9]

The *9/11 Commission Report* stated the appropriate response clearly:

> Bin Laden and Islamist terrorists mean exactly what they say: To them America is the font of all evil, the

"head of the snake, and it must be converted or destroyed."[10]

The only way to keep ahead of so many insidious threats is to have a strongly restored intelligence system, by means of which we can employ defensive procedures, alert the population, and actually make strategic preemptive strikes based on the intelligence that has been obtained.

We have already seen how easy it is for terrorists to come into the United States. To back up the efforts of the intelligence community, our homeland defense buildup needs to include a drastic buildup in our border patrol system and an unparalleled increase in the size of the FBI and the Coast Guard. We also need to continue to cooperate with international anti-crime organizations such as Interpol.

In addition to all preparedness measures, our domestic safety and our long-term survival as a free nation depend upon improving our ability to communicate and cooperate with each other. Political infighting only increases our vulnerability.

Secure and Free

National security, in all its ramifications, is an enormous undertaking. Is it possible to simultaneously build up, redeploy, and maintain a strong military force, protect our borders on land and sea, make calculated preemptive strikes wherever we see significant threats—and to continue to lead the civilized world morally and economically? Can we do it? The first step is to recognize and accept the challenge.

To win the long war ahead of us, we need to agree to focus our attention on making sweeping changes in our outdated capabilities. We need to identify strategic weaknesses as quickly as possible so that we can remedy them. And we need to recognize that the War on Terror is going to be a long one.

Wars that are worthwhile are always costly and frequently long, especially when they must be fought on so many fronts. The Cold War lasted more than forty years. World War II cost 405,399 American lives and involved major sacrifice from every citizen.[11] For my part, I am committed to this effort for the long haul, even when we go into overtime. I want my nation to be fully prepared and equally dedicated to the mission, with all that it will require.

CHAPTER 11

FULL SPEED AHEAD

REGARDLESS OF WHETHER OR NOT YOU AGREE WITH EVERYTHING I HAVE PUT FORWARD IN THESE PAGES, I HOPE THE BOOK HAS MADE YOU *THINK*. ALL OF MY OPINIONS ABOUT THE ISSUES THAT AFFECT THE UNITED STATES AND ALL OF MY PROPOSED STRATEGIES AND SOLUTIONS TO THE CHALLENGES FACING THE FEDERAL GOVERNMENT CENTER DOWN ON ONE THING—BASIC, THOUGHTFUL, COMMON SENSE.

A good legislator possesses an innovative kind of common sense that can be applied to the ever-developing challenges of nationhood in the twenty-first century as well as an appreciation for the moral principles that undergirded the Founding Fathers' establishment of this country. A good legislator is aware of public opinion but is not unduly swayed by it. Such a person is a practical and sensible individual both in private and in the arena of public service, and voters recognize and reward him or her with their trust.

My primary message in this book is simple: whatever you do with your own vote and however you are able to persuade the people around you to vote, I want you to use your own common sense and become a *thinking* voter, not someone who is moving in lockstep with others simply because of blind loyalty to family, race, political party, or neighborhood.

Think about it; look at the results of various approaches to societal problems. Which ones have worked? Which ones have become self-perpetuating sinkholes for human effort? Who set in motion the wheels of change? In other words, who should have the credit—or the blame—for something? Almost always, a little digging and a little thinking will reveal that the congratulations or the blame need to be shared with a previous administration. Such knowledge is a good cure for knee-jerk reactions—and a good reason to take a long look at the bigger picture. When it comes down to issues that affect your daily life, which political party best represents your interests and presents a workable, balanced approach to making progress?

All the issues are interrelated. You can't "vote your

pocketbook" or be a one-issue voter. You need to consider the ramifications. Picture a traditional "scales of justice." Balance is achieved when the weight that is placed into the right side equals the weight put into the left. Similarly, balance is achieved in the government of a society when the weight that is given to a particular methodology is counterbalanced by the weight of its outcome.

Only a thinking person will recognize the full import of a decision. A rationale that may appeal on the surface may incorporate a hidden flaw that will eventually undermine all its superficial attraction.

Charity Begins at Home

Speaking from my personal experience as a pastor who has initiated and maintained effective, major outreaches to needy people, I do not think that the liberals should get all the credit for taking care of people's needs. I certainly don't believe that the expression "compassionate conservative" is an oxymoron. As a conservative, I *think* about the results of public policies on people's lives, and I *care* about what happens to them.

In the past seven years alone, my church has fed and clothed more than 100,000 people. We operate a transitional home for women between the ages of eighteen and twenty-two who need assistance and direction in getting back on their feet and staying off the street. We create new outreaches based on the needs of our community and region. In implementing these outreaches,

177

we make observations about the crying needs around us within the framework of the broader economic and moral situation, and then we create programs that are far more than stopgaps—they are designed to not only meet immediate and urgent needs, but also to redeem difficulties in an identifiable and permanent way.

Bleeding-Heart Liberals

I suspect that it's not for nothing that we have the expression "bleeding-heart liberals." Liberals tend to approach the world with passionate conviction, all the while thinking with their hearts instead of their heads, although you can't see that at first. As a result, liberals present an agenda that may have a great deal of immediate appeal.

For example: "Stop the war and stop the killing!" Well, what normal person doesn't deplore killing? Yes, it would be good not to go to war. But what if this world does not happen to be a utopia? What if there are malicious enemies who would like to see us wiped out? What if those enemies are growing in strength as we speak? Shall we let them?

Another example: "Let a pregnant woman decide for herself—it's her own body!" She has a *right,* doesn't she? To what? To kill her baby, who has no say about his or her own rights to life or safety, and certainly no influence over the mother's choice to risk pregnancy in the first place?

Every thinking adult should be able to see that

morals and ethics do matter, and that they are not limited to the easy-to-agree-about categories such as crime. Conservatives, especially the Christian ones, suffer from repeated black eyes when they dare to introduce personal morals into a discussion.

Conservatives bring up such *touchy* issues. Gay marriage. Abortion. Come *on*—join the twenty-first century! This is the enlightened Western world. "Everyone" knows that everything goes. That stuff is OK. It doesn't hurt anybody.

Oh?

All right, if everything goes, then let's just keep saying "One nation, under God" in the pledge of allegiance. That should be pretty innocuous. It won't bother anyone over there on the Left, will it?

I think I see some smoke and mirrors over there.

Twenty-first-Century Thinking

I like to make clean and clear distinctions. I'm not too worried about "spin." I resist muddled thinking. I am aware that this approach may offend some people.

But I don't want my children and grandchildren to inherit a nation where feel-good logic prevails. If the national news agencies and the entertainment industry persist in basing so much of what they offer on liberal assumptions, my grandchildren will find it difficult to become responsible, productive citizens. Twenty-first-century society is complex enough without handicapping them with confusion about behavioral norms and even gender.

I don't want to sit by and watch the nation go down for the count. I want to participate in the decision-making process from within the halls of government. But even without being a United States senator, I get to vote, and so do you. I want our votes to count for something.

I don't want to throw my vote away on a candidate or a platform that, in the long run, is shortsighted. I don't want cultural pressure to influence my vote. Even when I end up voting the same way as "they" do, I want to stop and think about the issues first. I want to be a thinking voter. Every citizen should participate in the democratic process—*thinking* the whole way.

There may well be some candidate in another party who better exemplifies moral principles. Which one would be the best one for your city, your state, or your nation? Look at the values of the candidates as well as their party affiliation. Be more loyal to the principles you stand for than to a label. Hold those principles with integrity.

At the same time, recognize that the political party to which a candidate belongs advocates a set of stated beliefs and a plan of action to which, presumably, the individual candidate subscribes.

Do use your common sense. Your vote should be based on your principles, and your principles should be based on your common sense.

If you are ready, do join me and the other thinking citizens who believe that the ideals expressed in this book hold the best hope for our future as a nation.

Chapter 1
Black and Republican

1. *Republican Platform,* adopted by the Republican National Convention, July 15, 1980, Detroit, Michigan. Text at The American Presidency Project, Document Archive, http://www.presidency.ucsb.edu/showplatforms .php?platindex=R1980 (accessed September 15, 2005).

2. Ibid.

3. Ibid.

4. John Quincy Adams, *The Hingham Patriot* (Hingham, MA), June 29, 1839. Reprinted in the Timothy Hughes Rare & Early Newspapers catalog number 141 and quoted in David Barton, *American History in Black and White* (Aledo, TX: Wallbuilder Press, 2004), 17–18.

5. Barton, *American History in Black and White,* 49–50.

6. *Report of the Joint Select Committee to Inquire Into the Condition of Affairs in the Late Insurrectionary States* (New York: AMS Press, 1968), thirteen volumes.

7. Philip Mullins, *The Ancestors of George and Hazel Mullins,* chapter 12, "The Reconstruction Years: 1865–1900," http://uts.cc.utexas.edu/~pmullins/chapter12.htm (accessed November 17, 2005).

8. Frederick Douglass, *The Frederick Douglass Papers,* John Blassingame, editor (New Haven: Yale University Press, 1982), 385–386, from "What to the Slave Is the Fourth of

July?", July 5, 1852. As quoted in Barton, *American History in Black and White*, 11.

9. *Journal of the House of Representatives of the United States of America* (Washington: Government Printing Office, 1866), Vol. 63, 833–834, "June 13, 1866"; *Journal of the Senate of the United States of America* (Washington: Government Printing Office, 1866), Vol. 58, 505, "June 8, 1866," as quoted in Barton, *American History in Black and White*, 53.

10. Nancy Weiss, *Farewell to the Party of Lincoln* (Princeton, NJ: Princeton University Press, 1983), 100–236.

11. Theodore H. White, "The Negro Voter: Can He Elect a President?" *Collier's*, August 17, 1956, 19. Accessed at History Matters: The U.S. Survey Course on the Web, http://historymatters.gmu.edu/search.php?function=print&id =6331 (accessed November 17, 2005).

12. See *Congressional Record, 80th Congress, 2d Session* (Washington: Government Printing Office, 1948), Vol. 94, 927–929, February 2, 1948. See also Documentary History of the Truman Presidency, "The Truman Administration's Civil Rights Program: President Truman's Attempts to Put the Principles of Racial Justice into Law, 1948–1950," http://www .lexisnexis.com/academic/2upa/Aph/truman_docs/guide_ intros/tru12.htm.

13. White, "The Negro Voter: Can He Elect a President?"

14. *Congressional Quarterly* (Washington DC: Congressional Quarterly Service, 1965), Vol. 20, 606, 696, 88th Congress, 2d Session, vote on Civil Rights Bill of 1964, February 10, 1964. See also "Civil Rights Filibuster Ended," June 10, 1964, on Web site of U.S. Senate Historical Office at www.senate.gov/artandhistory/history/minute/ Civil_Rights_Filibuster_Ended.htm (accessed November 17, 2005) and "Backgrounder on the Civil Rights Act, U.S. State Department Information Services, http://usinfo.state

.gov/usa/infousa/facts/democrac/39.htm (accessed
November 17, 2005).

Title II, sec. 202 contains the heart of the Civil Rights
Act. It reads as follows:

"Sec 202. All persons shall be entitled to be free, at any
establishment or place, from discrimination or segregation
of any kind on the ground of race, color, religion, or national
origin, if such discrimination or segregation is or purports
to be required by any law, statute, ordinance, regulation,
rule, or order of a State or any agency or political subdivision
thereof." [Source: U.S. Statutes at Large 78 (1964): 241.]

Chapter 2
The Morality Connection

1. Proverbs 29:2, NRSV.

2. *Engel v. Vitale,* 370 U.S. 421, 430 (1962).

3. The Declaration of Independence, The National
Archives, http://www.archives.gov/national-archives
-experience/charters/declaration_transcript.html (accessed
November 18, 2005).

4. Ibid.

5. John Adams, *Works,* (1856), Vol. X, 45, to Thomas
Jefferson on June 28, 1813.

6. Benjamin Rush, "Of the Mode of Education Proper
in a Republic," *Essays, Literary, Moral and Philosophical*
(Philadelphia: Thomas and Samuel F. Bradford, 1798), 8.

7. "First Great Seal Committee—July 1776; Creating the
Great Seal of the United States 1776 to 1782," http://www
.greatseal.com/committees/firstcomm/index.html (accessed
November 18, 2005).

8. "Great Seal Mottoes: Annuit Cœptis," http://www .greatseal.com/mottoes/coeptis.html (accessed November 18, 2005).

9. George Washington, *Address of George Washington, President of the United States, and Late Commander in Chief of the American Army, to the People of the United States, Preparatory to His Declination* (Baltimore: George and Henry S. Keatinge, 1796), 22–23.

10. Full text can be found at "Jefferson's Wall of Separation Letter," http://www.usconstitution.net/jeffwall .html (accessed November 18, 2005).

11. See, for instance, *Reynolds v. U.S.*, 98 U.S. 145, 164 (1878).

12. *Engel v. Vitale,* 370 U.S. 421 (1962).

13. As quoted by Congressman Ernest J. Istook Jr. (R-OK), author of the Religious Freedom Amendment, in a press release dated June 27, 2005, http://www.house.gov/istook/ religiousfreedom/documents/rel2005_RFA1.pdf (accessed November 18, 2005). The revised text of the proposed Religious Freedom Amendment is as follows (can be seen at http://www.house.gov/istook/religiousfreedom/rqa.htm):
"To secure the people's right to acknowledge God according to the dictates of conscience:

"Neither the United States nor any State shall establish any official religion, but the people's right to pray and to recognize their religious beliefs, heritage, and traditions on public property, including schools, shall not be infringed.

"The United States and the States shall not compose school prayers, nor require any person to join in prayer or other religious activities."

14. John Adams, "To the Officers of the First Brigade of the Third Division of the Militia of Massachusetts on October 11, 1798," *The Works of John Adams, Second President*

of the United States, Charles Francis Adams, editor (Boston: Little, Brown, and Company, 1854), Vol. IX, 229.

Chapter 3
In Defense of Life

1. National Right to Life, "Abortion in the United States: Statistics and Trends," http://www.nrlc.org/abortion/facts/abortionstats.html; see also, http://www.cdc.gov/nchs/hus.htm and http://www.agi-usa.org/sections/abortion.php (all accessed September 27, 2005).

2. Statistics Canada, http://www.statcan.ca/Daily/English/050928/d050928a.htm (accessed September 27, 2005).

3. U.S. Census Bureau, http://factfinder.census.gov/servlet/SAFFPopulation?_event=Search&_name=&_state=04000US26&_county=&_cityTown=&_zip=&_sse=on&_lang=en&pctxt=fph (accessed September 27, 2005).

4. *Dred Scott v. Sandford,* 60 U.S. 407 (1856).

5. The complete text of the Republican Party platform of 1860 can be found at http://www.civilwarinteractive.com/DocsRepubPlatform1860.htm.

6. See the High Impact Leadership Coalition Web site at http://www.himpactus.com.

Chapter 4
A Tax *Solution?*

1. From a speech to the Convention of the National Federation of Independent Businessmen, June 21, 1987, Washington DC, transcribed in *Advancing the American Idea into the 90s* (Campaign for a New Majority State, 1988), 1.

2. As cited by Newt Gingrich in *Winning the Future: A 21st Century Contract with America* (Washington: Regnery, 2005), 129.

3. Excerpted from U.S. Code Collection, Legal Information Institute at http://www4.law.cornell.edu/uscode/html/uscode26/usc_sec_26_00000015----000-.html (accessed November 19, 2005).

4. Steve Forbes, *Flat Tax Revolution* (Washington DC: Regnery, 2005), 63.

5. As cited in George Will, "Cut 55,000 Pages of Tax Rules and Watch the Economy Soar," *Washington Post,* March 30, 2005.

6. All statistics from Andrei Grecu, *Flat Tax—the British Case,* 2004, a mini-book filed electronically at http://www.adamsmith.org/pdf/flattax.pdf (accessed October 28, 2005).

7. Ibid.

Chapter 5
Winning the Immigration Wars

1. As cited in "USCIS Announces Backlog Elimination Update," Press Release of the U.S. Citizenship and Immigration Services, March 22, 2005, archived at http://usinfo.state.gov/gi/Archive/2005/Mar/25-737784.html (accessed October 12, 2005).

2. Michael Barone and Victor Hanson, "The Immigration Debate," *eJournal USA: Society & Values* (an electronic publication of the U.S. Department of State Bureau of International Information Programs (IIP)), December 2004, at http://usinfo.state.gov/journals/itsv/1204/ijse/barone.htm (accessed October 13, 2005).

3. As cited by Allison Tarmann in "Number of U.S. Undocumented Migrants Rises, but Policy Response Still

Lacking," Population Reference Bureau, April 2005, http://
www.prb.org/Template.cfm?Section=PRB&template=/
ContentManagement/ContentDisplay.cfm&ContentID=12344
(accessed October 14, 2005).

4. Ibid.

5. Audrey Singer, "The Changing Face of America," *eJournal USA: Society & Values,* December 2004, at http://usinfo
.state.gov/journals/itsv/1204/ijse/singer.htm (accessed
October 13, 2005).

6. Institute of Medicine, *Hidden Costs, Values Lost:
Uninsurance in America* (National Academies Press, June
17, 2003), as cited on Web site of the National Coalition on
Health Care, http://www.nchc.org/facts/coverage.shtml
(accessed October 14, 2005).

7. As quoted in "Immigrants Make Up a Growing Share
of U.S. Population Without Health Insurance, Study Finds,"
Press Release, Employee Benefit Research Institute, June 13,
2005. Text at http://www.ebri.org/publications/prel/index
.cfm?fa=prelDisp&content_id=3527 (accessed October 14,
2005).

8. Newt Gingrich and David Merritt, "Congress Should
Pay for Immigrants' Healthcare," *Miami Herald,* May 6, 2005,
archived at http://www.newt.org/index.php?src=news&
prid=1079&category=Opinion&PHPSESSID
=13a94a31f5b068ecf3ded6df70747162 (accessed October 14,
2005).

9. Statistics from Mortimer B. Zuckerman, "A Debt to
Ourselves," *U.S. News & World Report,* October 3, 2005, 60.

10. News Release, U.S. Immigration and Customs
Enforcement, "US-VISIT Stops Murderers, Pedophiles and
Immigration Violators from Entering the United States,
Through Biometrics and International Cooperation," May

17, 2005, archived at http://usinfo.state.gov/gi/Archive/2005/ May/19-588378.html (accessed October 12, 2005).

11. Cited in Tarmann, "Number of U.S. Undocumented Migrants Rises, but Policy Response Still Lacking."

12. Porter Goss, testimony before the Subcommittee on International Terrorism and Nonproliferation of the Committee on International Relations, House of Representatives, 109th Congress, Washington DC, April 14, 2005. Topic: "Averting Nuclear Terrorism." Found on page 8 of text printed for the use of the Committee on International Relations House of Representatives. Archived at http://commdocs.house.gov/committees/intlrel/hfa20649.000/hfa20649_0.HTM (accessed October 14, 2005).

13. News Release, U.S. Immigration and Customs Enforcement.

Chapter 6
Helping Fellow Americans

1. Zuckerman, "A Debt to Ourselves."

2. From chap. 9, "The Social Safety Net: Public Assistance and Health Care," *Portrait of the USA,* an e-book on the U.S. Department of State's Office of International Information Programs Web site (http://usinfo.state.gov/usa/infousa/facts/factover/ch9.htm).

3. Zuckerman, "A Debt to Ourselves."

4. For a list of state liaisons for faith-based Initiatives, see www.cpjustice.org/charitablechoice/faithbystate.

5. Statistics from the U.S. Department of State's Office of International Information Programs, "Compassion in Action: Producing Real Results for Americans Most in Need, White

House Fact Sheet, March 1, 2005, http://usinfo.state.gov/usa/
faith/fs030105.htm (accessed November 19, 2005).

6. Noted in an article by Peter Wallsten, "Bush to Seek
More Funding for Faith-Based Charities," *Los Angeles Times,*
July 26, 2005, archived by the Pew Forum on Religion and
Public Life at http://pewforum.org/news/display
.php?NewsID=5134 (accessed October 10, 2005).

7. Cited in by the U.S. Department of State's Office of
International Information Programs, 2003, at http://usinfo
.state.gov/usa/faith/s071603.htm (accessed October 10, 2005).

8. Ibid. Mission statement from the St. Stephen's
Community House Web site at http://www.saintstephensch
.org (accessed October 10, 2005).

9. Cited in an address by President George W. Bush,
March 1, 2005, Washington, DC. Full transcription appears
on White House Web site at http://www.whitehouse.gov/
news/releases/2005/03/20050301-4.html (accessed October
10, 2005).

10. For more information about Prison Fellowship
International, visit their Web site at http://www.pfi.org.

11. All statistics from "Criminal Justice Statistics,"
Prison Fellowship Newsroom, April 5, 2005, www
.demossnewspond.com/pf/presskit/generalstats.htm
(accessed October 10, 2005).

12. Cited in the U.S. Department of State's Office of
International Information Programs at http://usinfo.state
.gov/usa/faith/s071603.htm, 2003 (accessed October 10, 2005).

13. From chap. 9, "The Social Safety Net: Public
Assistance and Health Care," *Portrait of the USA*, on Web
site of the U.S. Department of State's Office of International
Information Programs (http://usinfo.state.gov/usa/infousa/
facts/factover/ch9.htm).

14. From an address by George W. Bush in Philadelphia, December 12, 2002. Full transcription available on the White House Web site at http://www.whitehouse.gov/news/releases/2002/12/20021212-3.html (accessed October 10, 2005).

Chapter 7
Education That Works

1. From a summary of the report found at USInfo.gov, a Web site maintained by the U.S. State Department, http://usinfo.state.gov/is/Archive_Index/Executive_Summary_of_U.S._Commission_on_National_Security_Report.html, updated July 20, 2004.

2. Statistic from the National Bureau of Economic Research, as quoted in Thomas Hargrove, "Ph.D.s in America on the Decline," Scripps Howard News Service, August 18, 2005.

3. Ibid.

4. From "Education at a Glance 2005: Tables," statistics collected by the Organisation for Economic Co-operation and Development, headquartered in Paris, France, http://www.oecd.org/document/11/0,2340,en_2649_37455_35321099_1_1_1_37455,00.html (accessed November 19, 2005).

5. Ibid.

6. Ibid.

7. Ibid.

8. As quoted in Ben Feller, education writer for the Associated Press, "Study: U.S. Losing Ground in Education," September 13, 2005.

9. Barry McGaw, "Education 2005–2006," brochure published by the Organisation for Economic Co-operation and Development, April 19, 2005.

10. Quoted in Michael Dobbs, "In a Global Test of Math Skills, U.S. Students Behind the Curve," *Washington Post,* December 7, 2004, page A01, accessed at http://www .washingtonpost.com/wp-dyn/articles/A41278-2004Dec6 .html.

11. See report by Carolyn Kleiner Butler, "Success in the City," *U.S. News and World Report* 139, October 3, 2005, 54–56.

12. Ibid., 56.

Chapter 8
Commonsense Legal Reform

1. Thomas Jefferson, *Writings of Thomas Jefferson,* Albert Ellery Bergh, ed. (Washington DC: The Thomas Jefferson Memorial Association, 1904), Vol. XV, 277 (1820).

2. Ibid., 331–332 (1821).

3. From text of speech of Senator Stephen A. Douglas, Chicago, Illinois, July 9, 1858. See Abraham Lincoln, *Political Debates Between Lincoln and Douglas* (Cleveland: Burrows Bros. Co., 1897); Bartleby.com, 2001, 25. www.bartleby .com/251/ (accessed October 19, 2005).

4. From text of second Bush-Kerry debate: on Abortion, Issues2002, http://www.issues2000.org/Archive/ Bush_Kerry_2_Abortion.htm (accessed October 19, 2005).

5. *Park Lane Hosiery Co. v. Shore;* 439 U.S. 322, 343-44 (1979), Rehnquist, J., dissenting.

6. The Constitution includes six direct or indirect references to a provision for the impeachment of Supreme Court justices. See, in the text of the U.S. Constitution: In Article I: Section 2, Paragraph 5; Section 3, paragraphs 6 and 7. In

Article II: Section 2, Paragraph 1; Section 4, Paragraph 1. In Article III: Section 1, Paragraph 1; Section 2, Paragraph 3.

7. U.S. Constitution, Article II, Section 4, Paragraph 1.

8. White House Press Release, February 18, 2005, "President Signs Class-Action Fairness Act of 2005." Text available at http://www.whitehouse.gov/news/releases/2005/02/20050218-11.html (accessed October 20, 2005).

9. Cited in a speech by President Bush on January 5, 2005, "Legal Reform: The High Costs of Lawsuit Abuse," Office of the White House Press Secretary, www.whitehouse.gov/news/releases/2005/01/20050105-2.html (accessed October 19, 2005).

10. Gingrich, *Winning the Future: A 21st Century Contract with America*, 79.

11. See Small Business Administration Office of Advocacy Press Release, August 18, 2005, http://www.sba.gov/advo/press/05-40.html (accessed October 20, 2005).

12. Dee-Ann Durbin, Associated Press, "Bush Talks About Asbestos Litigation During Trip to Michigan," *Detroit News,* January 7, 2005. Article archived at www.detnews.com/2005/autoinsider/0501/07/politics-53744.htm (accessed October 20, 2005).

13. Statistics from "Asbestos Liability," Insurance Information Institute, New York, October 2005, 3. Text at www.iii.org/media/hottopics/insurance/asbestos (accessed October 20, 2005).

14. Ibid., 3.

15. Ibid., 2.

16. Ibid., 1.

Chapter 9
Developing Energy Resources

1. Statistics cited on Arctic Power Web site at http://www.anwr.org (accessed September 22, 2005).

2. Cited in History of Pipeline on Alyeska Pipeline Service Company Web site at http://www.alyeska-pipe.com/PipelineFacts/pipelineconstruction.html (accessed September 13, 2005).

3. Statistics cited on Arctic Power Web site at http://www.anwr.org (accessed September 22, 2005).

4. As quoted by Mark Clayton, "A Push to Build New U.S. Refineries," *Christian Science Monitor,* September 21, 2005, accessed online at http://www.csmonitor.com/2005/0921/p11s02-usec.html on September 23, 2005.

5. Ibid.

6. As quoted by Mike Simonson, "Ban on Great Lakes Drilling Made Permanent; Included in Energy Bill Signed This Week," KUWS radio (Wisconsin), published online August 9, 2005 at http://www.greatlakesdirectory.org/wi/080805_great_lakes.htm (accessed September 22, 2005).

7. From the Web site of the United States Coast Guard Office of Operating and Environmental Standards, http://www.uscg.mil/hq/g-m/mso/ans.htm (accessed September 23, 2005).

8. Sandra Turnbull, Sinem Akgun, John Blanchard, Jaiye Bridges, Rahul Burde, Debate, University of Michigan, 2002: "Yucca Mountain: The Argument for Its Use as a Permanent Nuclear Waste Repository," http://www.engin.umich.edu/class/ners211/project2002/pro/terrorism.html (accessed November 9, 2005).

9. Alliance for the Great Lakes, *An Advocate's Field Guide to Protecting Lake Michigan,* Chapter 2: "Stopping Toxic

Pollution to Lake Michigan," http://www.lakemichigan.org/field_guide/toxic_nuke.asp (accessed November 19, 2005).

10. Ed "Redwood" Ring, "Hydrogen Fuel Cell Cars," December 4, 2000, California Fuel Cell Partnership, http://www.fuelcellpartnership.org (accessed November 9, 2005).

Chapter 10
Countering Global Threats

1. Quoted in "Al-Qaida Vows Anti-US Attacks," published on September 10, 2003 English edition of the Arab news site, Al-jazeera.net, http://66.102.7.104/search?q=cache:gJP3xNx1HIQJ:english.aljazeera.net/NR/exeres/51BD3065-02EA-45FD-ABC6-072FD3816E25.htm++site:english.aljazeera.net+Al-Zawahri&hl=en (accessed October 17, 2005).

2. George W. Bush, Statement on National Security, September 17, 2002. Full text at http://www.whitehouse.gov/nsc/nssall.html (accessed October 12, 2005).

3. George W. Bush, "U.S. Air Force Commencement Address," June 2, 2004. Full text at http://www.whitehouse.gov/news/releases/2004/06/20040603.html (accessed November 19, 2005).

4. Fact Sheet: President Bush Remarks on the War on Terror, Office of the White House Press Secretary, October 6, 2005, http://www.whitehouse.gov/news/releases/2005/10/20051006-2.html (accessed October 17, 2005).

5. *The 9/11 Commission Report: Final Report of the National Commission on Terrorist Attacks Upon the United States* (New York: W. W. Norton, 2004), 105.

6. Bush, Statement on National Security.

7. This concept comes from Thomas McInerney and Paul Vallely, *Endgame: The Blueprint for Victory in the War on Terror* (Washington DC: Regnery, 2004).

8. Franklin D. Roosevelt, September 11, 1941. Recording of the full fireside chat found at http://www.archives.gov/research/ww2/sound-recordings.html.

9. Quoted in "Al-Qaida Leader Warns of New Attacks," published on February 24, 2004 English edition of the Arab news site, Al-jazeera.net, http://66.102.7.104/search?q =cache:qAClAReX4ScJ:english.aljazeera.net/NR/exeres/ B4281D01-ABE9-4425-8A6B-686752B4242C.htm++site :english.aljazeera.net+Al-Zawahri&hl=en (accessed October 17, 2005).

10. The *9/11 Commission Report*, 362.

11. History News Network, http://hnn.us/articles/1381 .html (accessed October 26, 2005).

INDEX

9/11 20, 80, 114, 156, 159, 167, 171
9/11 Commission Report 166, 172

A

abortion 4, 35–39, 42, 47, 71, 179
  slavery and 42
Adams, John Quincy 8
Afghanistan 169
African American(s) 1–2, 6, 10, 12–14, 46–47, 85, 93
Al-Arabiya 162
Al-Jazeera 162
Al-Qaeda 162, 164
al-Zawahiri, Ayman 160, 172
Alan Guttmacher Institute 35
Angel Tree 99
Arctic National Wildlife Refuge (ANWR) 138–139, 141–145
assistance, public 62, 87, 100
Association Health Plans (AHPs) 131–132

B

balance of power 122
bankruptcy 126, 133
Bill of Rights 28, 31
bin Laden, Osama 166, 172
black(s) 1–2, 4, 6–12, 14–15, 40, 42, 47, 70, 72, 120–121
  black vote 2, 15
Black Contract with America on Moral Values 47–48
border patrol 77, 173
Broad Prize for Urban Education 110
Brooke, Sen. Edward 15

Bruce, Sen. Blanche K. 15

Bush, President George W. 20, 67, 93, 95, 102, 121, 124, 127, 138, 149, 152, 160, 170, 172

business (corporate) 22, 51–55, 59, 61, 63, 67, 72, 126, 128, 131–132, 134, 136, 146, 156

   overseas 54–55, 63, 126

Butler, Deborah 15

C

Center for Justice and Reconciliation 99

Centers for Disease Control and Prevention 35

Central Intelligence Agency (CIA) 80, 166–167

charity(ies) 95, 102, 177

China 65, 105, 169

Christian(s), Christianity 24, 26, 28, 31, 40, 179

church(es) 6, 15–17, 31–32, 92–93, 98–99, 177

   and state, separation of 28–32

citizens, senior 96

Citizenship and Immigration Services 70

City Center Ministries 100

civil rights 2, 7, 11–14, 120–121

   Civil Rights Act 14

Civil War 7, 9, 12, 42, 121

Class–Action Fairness Act 127

Cleveland, Grover 12

Clinton, Bill 166

Coast Guard 149, 173

Cold War 166, 168, 170, 174

Colson, Chuck 99

Congress, United States 8, 10, 14, 29, 41–42, 46, 70, 76, 81, 86, 89, 95, 119, 121–122, 127–128, 132, 135, 138, 147, 166–167

Congressional Budget Office 64

conservative(s), conservatism 2, 47, 93, 124, 137, 165, 177, 179

Constitution, United States 10–11, 29–30, 33, 41–42, 56, 119–124
   Fifteenth Amendment 11, 121
   First Amendment 29–32
   Fourteenth Amendment 11, 70, 79
   Thirteenth Amendment 11, 121
   Three-Fifths Clause 10
Coolidge, Calvin 66
crime, criminal(s) 42, 78, 81, 83, 88, 97–99, 106, 123, 166, 173, 179

D

Danbury Baptist Association 29
Declaration of Independence 8, 25, 36, 56
defense, national 20, 165–166
democracy 5, 161, 164
Democratic Party 3, 6–7, 12, 14, 47
Department of Energy 146, 151
Department of Homeland Security 171
Department of Labor 100
Department of the Interior 141
Depression, Great 12
Detroit 1, 3, 15, 19, 139, 150
development, sustainable 156–157
diplomacy 161, 165–166
Douglas, Stephen A. 121
Douglass, Frederick 11
Dred Scott v. Sandford 40, 120–122
Dubois, W. E. B. 10

E

economy 3, 49–53, 55–56, 63, 66, 72, 103, 105–106, 144, 156
   economic growth 4, 50–53, 58, 66, 108, 154

economic policy 20

education 16, 20, 45–46, 59, 71–72, 88, 96, 98, 101, 103–115

    accountability and 108–111

    competition and 111–112

    portability and 112–113

    rankings, scores 24, 103, 106–107, 111, 115

Education Trust 108

Egypt 165

Eisenhower, Dwight 14

Employee Benefit Research Institute 74

employment 4, 53, 96

Energy Policy Act of 2005 152

energy resources 137–157

    alternative fuels 137, 152–155

    oil, natural gas 137–149, 152–153

entrepreneurs 38, 52–53

environmentalism 140–141, 145–149

Establishment Clause 29

ethanol 153–154

Everson v. Board of Education 30

Exodus Transitional Community 100

F

Faith, Word of 17, 92–93

Faith-Based and Community Initiatives (FBCI) 93–94

family 5–6, 16, 22, 32, 43–47, 59, 62, 79, 85, 176

    and gay rights 43

    and marriage 46–47

    and taxes 45, 62

    traditional 43

Federal Bureau of Investigation (FBI) 173

Federal Communications Commission 89

Fish and Wildlife Service 141

Founding Fathers 8, 25–26, 42, 119, 176

Franklin, Benjamin 27

Frederick Douglass Community Development Corporation
    95

Fugitive Slave Law 8

G

Gingrich, Newt 47, 129

government, federal 14, 29, 64, 67, 75–76, 87, 89, 91, 93, 97,
    100, 102, 118, 122, 144, 160, 175

Great Britain 24–25, 163

Great Lakes 36, 147–152

Great Seal of the United States 27

H

Hart-Rudman Commission 104

Henry Ford High School 15

Hispanic Americans 4, 72, 76

housing, low-income 96

Humaita 100

Hussein, Saddam 166

hydrogen 148, 154

I

immigration 69–84, 114

    assimilation and 71, 73

    border security and 77–80

    health care and 74–76

    illegal 73–77, 80

    poverty and 76

    quotas 79–80

Immigration and Customs Enforcement Agency 82

Immigration and Naturalization Service 78

India 71
initiatives, faith-based 92–102
InnerChange Freedom Initiative 100
innovation *xi*, 50, 103
Iran 163–164, 170
Iraq 159, 164, 167, 169–170
Israel 27, 162

J

Jefferson, Thomas 7, 25–27, 29–30, 119–120
"Jim Crow" 12
jobs 20, 38, 53–55, 76–77, 100, 115, 140, 144, 157
 job creation 52, 65, 67, 126, 143
 job training 92, 100–101
Johnson, Lyndon 14
judges, justices 31, 36, 118–124, 127
justice 47, 127, 129, 177
 and righteousness 47
 restorative 99

K

Kemp, Jack 50, 53
Kemp-Roth Tax Act 50
Kennedy, Bobby 2
Kennedy, John F. (JFK) 2, 7, 14, 66
King, Martin Luther, Jr. 1, 10
Ku Klux Klan 9

L

Lake Taylor High School 110
lawsuits, frivolous 126, 128–129
lawyers, personal injury 126, 129–130

leadership, leaders *xi*, 21, 25–26, 32–33, 37, 47, 50–51, 84, 111, 160, 162–163, 165, 171–172

Levin, Sen. Carl 20

liberal(s), liberalism 12, 31, 43, 46, 54, 79, 81, 97, 124, 137, 166–167, 177–179

Libya 163

Lincoln, Abraham 4, 6–7, 13, 40, 42, 48, 120–121

M

Malcolm X 10

Medicaid 86, 90–92

Medicare 62, 85, 90–92

methanol 153–154, 157

Mexico 64, 73, 75, 77–80

Miami Herald 75

Michigan 14, 17, 20, 36, 44, 53–54, 112, 133, 139, 147, 149, 151, 155–156

and the Great Lakes 147–149

Southfield 16, 133

University of 16

Middle East 70, 161, 164–165, 170

Migration Policy Institute 73

military 32, 51, 59, 77, 115, 161, 168–171, 173

spending 169

strength 165, 169

Missouri Compromise 8

morality 23, 26, 28, 32–33

government and 22–24, 28

moral consequences 24

moral integrity 20–24

moral principles 22–23, 28, 46, 176, 180

moral values 32–33, 43, 48

Moseley-Braun, Sen. Carol 15

Musharraf, President 164

N

National Association for the Advancement of Colored People
    13
National Endowment for Democracy 162
New Deal 12–14
No Child Left Behind Act 109
North Korea 170
Nuclear Waste Policy Act 151

O

Oakland Community College 16
Obama, Sen. Barack 15
Operation New Hope 100
Organisation for Economic Co-operation and Development
    107
organizations, nonprofit 31, 59, 88, 98–99
outreach(es) (social) 17, 92–93, 177

P

Pakistan 71, 163– 164
Palestine 162
Peacemaker Family Center, The 96
platform (political) 3, 5, 40, 180
poll(s), opinion ix, 3, 81, 161–162
pollution, environmental 145, 149
poverty 4, 58, 76, 85, 87, 89
Powell, Adam Clayton, Jr. 14
power, nuclear 137, 151–152
power, solar 154
power, wind 154
Prison Fellowship 99–100

programs, government 86–87, 89, 100
Proliferation Security Initiative 163

R
RAND Institute for Civil Justice 134
Reagan, Ronald 3, 5–6, 66, 165, 168
recidivism 99–100
Reconstruction 9, 12
refineries 145–147, 149, 152
reform, legal 125
   and litigation costs 128
   and medical liability 130–131
reform, tort 124–125
   and asbestos litigation 133–134
Rehnquist, Chief Justice William 31, 123
religion 27–30, 32–33, 102, 167
Republican party, GOP 3, 5–7, 12, 40, 46–47, 53
   and Contract with America 47
   blacks and 6–15
   party of Lincoln 4, 6, 42
resources, domestic 153
Revels, Sen. Hiram R. 15
Revolutionary War 26
Roe v. Wade 35, 42, 121
Roosevelt, Franklin D. 12–13, 170
Rush, Benjamin 27

S
Saudi Arabia 165
schools 12, 22–23, 31, 35, 88, 98, 107–110, 112–113, 115, 156
   charter 112–113
   private 45–46, 92, 112
   public 22–23, 31, 72, 112–114

security, domestic (national) (homeland) 20–21, 74, 80–81,
        83, 104–105, 114, 147, 160, 166, 168, 171, 173
Senate, United States 2, 11, 14–15, 20, 31, 43, 118, 123, 132
services, social 93–95, 102
slaves, slavery 7–9, 11, 23, 25, 40–42, 121–122
Small Business Health Fairness Act 132
Social Security 5, 13, 38–39, 61–62, 90
St. Stephen's Community House 96
standards, universal 155–156
State Department 27
systems, information 91, 168

T
Taiwan 169
Taliban 164
taxes 12, 20, 45, 49–55, 57, 61–66, 112, 144, 146–147
    alternative minimum tax 61
    avoidance 64
    brackets 60
    capital gains 55, 67
    corporate 52, 54, 61
    death 55, 61
    Earned Income Tax Credit 62, 86
    exemptions 59, 62, 102
    flat tax 52, 60–67
    personal 60–61, 66
    taxation without representation 24
teacher specialists 113–114
terrorism, terrorists 21, 73, 80, 104, 151, 156, 159–164, 167,
        170, 172–173
Truman, Harry 13

U

U.S. Supreme Court 30–31, 35–37, 40, 112, 118–124
United Nations 99
US-VISIT (United States Visitor and Immigrant Status
    Indicator Technology) 78, 81–83
utilities 155–156

V

volunteerism 101
vouchers, school 112

W

wage, minimum 89
Wallace v. Jaffree 31
Washington, George 28
waste, nuclear 151
weapons 163, 167–172
    biological 171–172
    nuclear 80–81, 163, 171–172
    of mass destruction 104, 163, 167
White, Theodore H. 13
whites, southern 9, 12, 14
Wilkins, Roy 13
World War II 19, 38, 174

Y

Yucca Mountain 151